D1598166

The Management of
Labor Unions

Emerging Issues in Employee Relations
John T. Dunlop and Arnold M. Zack, Editors

Grievance Arbitration
Issues on the Merits in Discipline, Discharge, and Contract Interpretation
Arnold M. Zack

The Management of Labor Unions
Strategic Planning in Historical Constraints
John T. Dunlop

The Management of Labor Unions

*Decision Making with
Historical Constraints*

John T. Dunlop
Harvard University

Lexington Books
D.C. Heath and Company/Lexington, Massachusetts/Toronto

Library of Congress Cataloging-in-Publication Data
Dunlop, John Thomas, 1914–
   The management of labor unions.

   1. Trade-unions—United States—Management.
I. Title.
HD6508.D86   1989   331.88'068   89-8273
ISBN 0-669-21143-5

Published simultaneously in Canada
Printed in the United States of America
International Standard Book Number: 0-669-21143-5
Library of Congress Catalog Card Number: 89-8273

The paper used in this publication meets the minimum requirements of American National Standard for Information Sciences—Permanence of Paper for Printed Library Materials, ANSI Z39.48-1984. ∞™

Year and number of this printing:

89   90   91   92   10   9   8   7   6   5   4   3   2   1

Contents

Tables

Preface

To some, the title of this book—*The Management of Labor Unions*—is an oxymoron in linking the rationality of management with the emotion of mass organizations and the legacy of history. The problems that confronted an earlier labor movement may not have involved a significant management component as it sought to define its identity, its membership, its methods, its relations to the rest of American society, and its ideology by a trial and error process. But contemporary labor unions face issues more akin to those that concern a wide range of other organizations in defining their operational goals, maintaining internal coherence, utilizing scarce resources, developing policies and personnel, relating to other groups, and dealing with governments.

The chapters, cases, questions, and suggested readings of this book are premised on the experience that there is much to be learned, and to be taught, from a perspective that compares and contrasts the governance of major categories of organizations in American society: business, government, education, nonprofit organizations generally and labor unions. The role of executives and leaders and their relations to constituents and members in different organizations and environments is illuminated by a comparative approach.

These insights and analytical perspectives provide issues of both substance and process for students of business, public policy, and voluntary organizations generally just as they raise questions for labor union officers. The themes of common elements and variable characteristics across executives in different types of organizations pervade part I, which focuses on the management function.

But no one, in my experience, can well appreciate the operation of a large modern organization or the role of its executives solely with the analytical tools of a discipline or a hybrid of disciplines and models. The course of development of an institution over time often has shaped and constrained significantly its internal goals and priorities, its patterns of leadership, its structure and governance, and its methods of adaptation to external challenges and changes. Part II focuses on the institutional development of labor organizations in the United States, internally and from restraints imposed by the larger society, as both forces have shaped the setting for contemporary decision making. The legacy of history rather than the present environment or current leaders influences many decisions in all organizations.[1]

The attitudes and philosophy of labor organizations toward surrounding communities and the larger society and their interactions is the subject of Part III. The changing articulation of these views and values is reflected in the statements of leadership.

This book constitutes a long-term interest in decision making in a variety of categories of organizations, and in specific institutions, reflected in writing and teaching on the analytics of decisions[2] and their historical evolution.[3] It also reflects the interchanges with countless students in courses in Harvard University's School of Business Administration and School of Government, with undergraduates and graduate students, as well as generations of Harvard Trade Union Fellows drawn from labor organizations since 1942.

The perspective of a case or a problem presented in the framework of one organization, say a union, often illuminates the issues confronting other organizations with which it interacts, say a business or a government agency. Discipline meted out by business management may create issues of fair representation for a union; a decision by a labor organization to strike poses issues to a management. Strategic planning by a labor organization can be operative only with a measure of synchronization with directly related business and public plans. Attention to this interdependence of decision making among various types of organizations is encouraged by the initial emphasis in part I on the management function across organizations.

I am indebted to Professor Morris A. Horowitz, chairman of the Department of Economics, Northeastern University, and a colleague in dispute resolution for assisting in the development of some case materials used in this book. Fiona Laird served as a research assistant in 1986 and helped to gather and organize some of the materials for the cases.

Marie Stroud typed the manuscript and helped to see it through to publication while coordinating gently and effectively a variety of diffuse office responsibilities.

Notes

1. See Richard E. Neustadt and Ernest R. May, *Thinking in Time, The Uses of History for Decision Makers* (New York: The Free Press, 1986).
2. In my *Wage Determination Under Trade Unions* (New York: Macmillan Company, 1944, pp. 28–121) the analysis developed a set of objectives that a labor organization, with the range of preferences of those it represented, might choose to maximize. This discussion set in motion a dialogue that still continues. See, for in-

stance, J. Pemberton, "A 'Managerial' Model of the Trade Union," *Economic Journal,* September 1988, pp. 755–71.

In the 1950s and 1960s in contrast to the almost total academic preoccupation of the period with "union democracy," it seemed important to raise questions of organizational goals, collective bargaining strategy, internal information systems, personnel policy, and efficiency. See, "What's Ahead in Union Government," Joel Seidman, ed., *Trade Union Government and Collective Bargaining, Some Critical Issues* (New York: Praeger Publishers, 1970, pp. 198–206). The discussion was prepared for a conference November 16–18, 1967. These ideas were more fully developed and illustrated in *Labor and the American Community,* with Derek C. Bok (New York: Simon and Schuster, 1970, pp. 64–188). Also see Malcolm S. Salter and John T. Dunlop, *Industrial Governance and Corporate Performance, An Introductory Essay,* (Boston: Harvard Business School, 1989).

3. See John T. Dunlop, "The Development of Labor Organization: A Theoretical Framework," *Insights Into Labor Issues,* R.A. Lester and Joseph Shister, Eds. (New York: The Macmillan Company, 1948), pp. 163–93. The fifty volumes in the Wertheim Publications in Industrial Relations trace in detail the institutional development of particular national unions, state federations, labor-management relations in various sectors, and the industrial relations systems of various countries.

Part I
The Management Function

1
The Management of Organizations

In the view of classical economists, from Adam Smith through John Stuart Mill, an economy is comprised of individual citizens, small, independent producing or trading enterprises and farms, and the state. Much of our theory of economics, earlier called political economy, and political theory were developed with this simplified view of society.[1] There was no room for intermediate bodies such as labor organizations, trade associations, or non-profit entities, and any organization suspect of exercising coercive or restrictive powers against the rest of the community was automatically seen as antisocial.

But today we live in a society with thousands of intermediate organizations to perform specified functions and achieve personal, group, and communal objectives. We are much more than a society of individuals, small enterprises, and the traditional state. Educational institutions, health care organizations, labor unions, professional societies, farm organizations, foundations, community groups and voluntary services, and others are illustrative, and our distinctive large business enterprises and complex government agencies have no earlier counterpart. Moreover, we have developed hybrid private-public organizations and partnerships that diffuse responsibilities.[2] Through their officers and members, such organizations interact with each other in markets and through governmental processes, the press and media, and community channels.

It is incumbent on all those who seek to understand the modern multi-organization economy, and those who aspire to posts in the leadership or management of any one of them, to devote serious time to their internal processes, complex interactions, and historical development.

Analysis and Organizational Development

In approaching any of the categories of organizations noted, it is rewarding (1) to seek to understand the decision-making processes in organizations generally and in the particular class such as business, government, or labor, and (2) to appreciate the development of the category of organizations and the particular case—and how it came to acquire its dominant current features. The first exercise is analytical and abstract in its method; it draws on microeconomic theory, business strategic and financial planning, and sociological theories.[3] The second is an assignment in historical development with a sensitivity to the evolving environment, the characteristics of the constituencies, the legal framework, the role and influence of the larger society, and the processes of internal organizational change. This attention to organizational development is not the concern of a single discipline but rather is an informed eclectic creation.

For some of the major types of organizations in American society, it may be appropriate to cite for each a book that provides the sort of historical background that gives understanding to its current features and to its interactions—cooperation and conflicts—with other major organizations and particularly with governments.

> For business enterprises: Alfred D. Chandler, Jr., *The Visible Hand, The Managerial Revolution in American Business* (Cambridge: Belknap Press of Harvard University Press, 1977).

> For health care organizations: Paul Starr, *The Social Transformation of American Medicine* (New York, Basic Books, 1982).

> For higher education institutions: Derek Bok, *Higher Learning* (Cambridge: Harvard University Press, 1986).

> For government regulatory agencies: Thomas K. McCraw, *Prophets of Regulation* (Cambridge: Belknap Press of Harvard University Press, 1984).

> For labor organizations: Lloyd Ulman, *The Rise of the National Trade Union: The Development and Significance of the Structure, Governing Institutions, and Economic Policies* (Cambridge: Harvard University Press, 1966).

Such historical settings provide an essential constraint and perspective to attempts to explain or even to provide normative standards for the decision-making processes of organizations solely by deductive logic and formal models. Analytical tools do contribute significant insights into the operations of some organizations, such as large-scale business enterprises, and the extension of the approach to other types of organizations can be helpful in some respects. These techniques need to be mastered, evaluated, and applied with judgment. But the historical setting of institutional development ensures against what Alfred North Whitehead called the "fallacy of misplaced concreteness," the tendency to treat the model and its deductions as the real world rather than as an abstraction.

The resort to analytical tools combined with the study of institutions, and their interaction, that is recommended here is akin to steering between Scylla and Charybdis, between the elegance of deductive models and the perversity of reality. Either course without concern for the other can be treacherous.

Practitioners tend to reflect on their experience, and even pass on to the younger generations, certain rules of thumb or precepts that embody principles that are neither isolated facts nor formal theories, but they are often the beginnings of a form of analysis. Consider the following:

- Informal methods of administration that work well in a small organization often tend to become unsatisfactory as the organization grows in complexity and size. More formal techniques and information flows are then required for decisions and supervision.
- The structure of an organization needs to be evaluated periodically to ensure that it fits the current goals.
- When organizations grow large, it becomes important to develop an explicit planning process. Although methods differ in sophistication, a conscious effort should be made to define goals and appraise progress toward them.
- After plans are established, it is generally helpful to establish an operating budget that reflects how resources are to be allocated among the various programs, activities, or units of the organization.
- An operating budget serves the function of informing subordinate officials of some of the goals they are expected to accomplish in the ensuing period.
- An environment is sought in the organization that minimizes conflicts between the goals of the organization and those of the individuals who work in it.
- To develop an effective organization, the systematic recruitment and training of potential leadership at all levels is essential.

Such rules of thumb—or call them principles—are little more than common sense, and most leaders or executives of organizations are well aware of them or similar lessons of experience. The pressures of limited financial resources have compelled most serious executives to consider various alternative means of using staff and resources more effectively to achieve their organizational goals.

Practitioners from organizations that have a relatively high degree of "political" content to decisions or in which "political" influences exert a heavy role in the process often contend that modern management techniques such as strategic planning, program budgeting, and cost effectiveness are not readily transplanted to their organization. These views have often been expressed with regard to government agencies, labor organizations, and educational institutions. There is undoubtedly a degree of contrast between some of these organizations and many businesses. The infusion of political considerations (internal or external to the organization) or the extension of majority vote to every decision may well constrain considerations of efficiency and long-term effective performance.

But it would be idle to insist that useful management choices at the margin, even in a heavy political environment, are not vital to the achievement of organizational goals under the chronic conditions of a shortage of resources. Consider, for example, whether to add or subtract five staff members, to open or to close a department, to take an internal poll of views of members prior to negotiations, or to install a computer system for operations. Such issues call for a sharper definition of goals, priorities among an array of desirable objectives, some comparisons of costs and future benefits, the careful selection and training of personnel—in brief some degree of executive planning and decisionmaking within the established political environment. The management techniques may be based on back-of-the envelope estimates, an outside consultant, or more elaborate internal processes, but these sorts of decisions come to call for a major management component even in a setting saturated with political considerations that are weighed in the decision-making process.

Labor Organizations

A review of labor unions in the United States by "management consultants" would be likely to conclude that until recently little effort has been devoted, and only in a few organizations, to long-range planning, to establishing procedures for budgeting, seeking to attract the ablest men and women to office and to staff positions, to establish an effective communications system up and down the organization with reliable feedback, to consider adaptations in structure suitable to new problems and opportunities, or to seek outside research support from private foundations on issues of union policy. Such judgments, it would often be responded, do not sufficiently recognize the political qualities of a labor organization and its leadership or administration.

But the difficult environment that has confronted American unions—in collective bargaining, in legislative and administrative issues with government, the courts, and public opinion—during the past decade has stimulated considerable study, review, and experimentation in new methods of management and administration.[4] The American Federation of Labor–Congress of Industrial Organizations (AFL-CIO) has instituted a budgetary process and telecommunication conferences on a national basis, created new training programs for staff, organized study sessions and seminars for the media and press, strengthened its community programs and visibility, and developed media spot programs. It has attracted younger, well-trained professional staff. In these newer activities, and AFL-CIO has been joined by a growing number of its major affiliates. A judgment on the effectiveness and outcomes of these newer methods must necessarily be deferred for a while.

All of these developments, some of which emerged in particular unions as long ago as several decades, do not mean that labor organizations are any less political.[5] Indeed the internal governance of unions has democratic values enshrined in values, constitutions, and statute that decree a bill of rights for members, election processes, financial reporting and oversight, limitations on supervision of subordinate bodies, and so forth and in the courts, which place on the union the complex duty of fair representation, to represent its members without hostile discrimination.[6]

These political processes place significant constraints on the leadership in treating issues of internal management and, although it is not the current primary concern, in dealing with business or public managements as well. These constraints avert the energies of leaders, weaken their control over subordinate organizations, interrupt continuity in office, and impede the raising of funds from dues or assessments. The political process leaves its mark on the selection and development of leaders; it tends to foreclose leadership from outside the organization and allows the administration little opportunity to influence the pool of local officials from which higher leadership tends to be drawn. More important still, the election process offers only slight assurance that executives will be chosen for their administrative or managerial talents. Moreover, many labor organizations have internal political problems that are sufficiently troublesome, or serious issues with employers, to preclude for the time being any sustained attack on basic internal administrative questions.

Nevertheless, an energetic labor leader is constrained to reflect carefully about the use of the organization's limited resources. It is difficult to achieve dues increases that are necessary to finance all of the desired activities. The intricacies of health and pension funds have exposed union officers to consultants using more advanced administrative techniques. The advent of computers has led to more elaborate ways of gathering, storing, and using more information. The AFL-CIO has helped to focus attention on managerial techniques.

As a result of these and other pressures, the methods of administration and management in American unions are a substantial improvement over those in use a generation ago. It is probably not unrealistic to expect a significant advance over the next decade or two within the political constraints briefly sketched.

This discussion of the management of labor organizations might well be largely out of place in a country in which labor unions' only objective was to seize political control or achieve electoral majority for a political party. In the United States the environment and the hard lessons of labor organizations created a dominant form that came to be known as business unionism.

The management of labor unions has been introduced in the context of a range of organizations that are major players in the society in order to facilitate comparisons and contrasts, to appreciate similarity and diveristy between labor unions and businesses, governmental agencies, educational institutions, voluntary hospitals, and other organizations, and to understand the roles of their executives. The next chapter elaborates this theme.

Notes

1. See Lionel Robbins, *The Theory of Economic Policy in English Classical Political Economy* (London: Macmillan, 1953), p. 105.

2. *American Society, Public and Private Responsibilities*, ed. Winthrop Knowlton and Richard Zeckhauser (Cambridge, Mass.: Ballinger, 1986).

3. See Kenneth R. Andrews, *The Concept of Corporate Strategy* (Homewood, Ill.: Dow Jones-Irwin, 1971); Michael E. Porter, *Competitive Strategy: Techniques for Analyzing Industries and Competitors* (New York: Free Press, 1980); and Anne L. Kalleberg and Ivar Berg, *Work and Industry, Structures, Markets and Processes* (New York: Plenum Press, 1987).

4. *The Changing Situation of Workers and Their Unions*, Report by the AFL-CIO Committee on the Evolution of Work (Washington, D.C.: AFL-CIO, 1985).

5. Derek C. Bok and John T. Dunlop, *Labor and the American Community* (New York: Simon and Schuster, 1970), pp. 138–188.

6. Labor-Management Reporting and Disclosure Act of 1959, Public Law 86-257. See *The Changing Law of Fair Representation*, ed. Jean T. McKelvey (Ithaca, N.Y.: IRL Press, 1985).

2
A Comparison of Executives in
Four Fields

Although modern methods of management have been applied most intensively in business enterprises, they have been adapted increasingly for use in governments, educational institutions, hospitals, and nonprofit organizations, particularly large ones. Two-year graduate programs now introduce these management tools not only to those seeking careers in business but also to candidates for positions in public policy, public health, education, the military, and administrative posts in religious and charitable organizations. Accordingly it is appropriate to explore whether these management and administrative techniques can be applied and used to advantage, and to what extend and, with what limitations, in the operation of labor organizations as well.

One way to explore these questions is to begin with a comparison of the role of executives in four different types of organizations: private business, government, academic administration, and labor organizations. The role of the labor executive is appreciated in the setting of a comparison and a contrast with the activities of executives in these other types of organizations.

Any such comparison among organizations involves some overlap since there are differences within each type: academic administration may be private or governmental and may include responsibility for housing and food service, hospital management, and complex scientific facilities; business executives may range from trade associations and nonprofit organizations through research bodies to general managers of diverse profit centers with varying degrees of governmental regulation; and government executives may encompass a vast scope from public business enterprises, such as the postal service, utilities, and defense installations, to broad policymaking and diverse regulatory agencies of federal, state, and local governments. To recognize the full continuum and common elements of executive activity in each of these

Adapted from Eli Ginzberg, ed., *Executive Talent, Developing and Keeping the Best People* (New York: John Wiley & Sons, Inc., 1988), pp. 117–142. © 1988 by Eli Ginzberg, Reprinted by permission of John Wiley & Sons, Inc.

fields is not to preclude attention to separate modal types provided it is recognized that some degree of abstraction is necessarily involved. Executives in the real world do not always behave as depicted for the analysis.

The focus of interest here is in administrative, executive, and leadership roles *within* organizations. The concern is not with isolated individuals who may have a significant impact on the larger society, albeit with an organizational home, as Nobel laureates in the sciences, potential saints and spiritual prophets, great writers of fiction, visionary political leaders, and charismatic figures in a movement. We are dealing with men and women who make their contribution and achieve their rewards *through* organizations in these four fields.

The observations that follow are confined to the United States. They do not necessarily apply to other countries. In France the *grandes écoles* such as Normale and Polytechnique and the University of Tokyo in Japan train a business and government leadership that has no counterpart here. The presidency of the American college and university is unique since in continental Europe and Latin America, the rector is confined within a narrow corridor between the power of the faculty guild and a government ministry in charge. In the Soviet Union the role of the party in the recruitment and designation of leadership in organizations is alien by American standards.

Common Elements among Executives in Four Fields

There appear to be certain common elements in executive performance among these fields, although the significance and weight attached to each varies widely among and within each (table 2–1).

Environmental Analysis

The executive needs to understand and articulate to the organization the environment within which it operates and the likely changes in that milieu in the short and longer periods ahead. At times the exterior world of the orga-

Table 2–1
Common Elements among Executives in Four Fields

1. Environmental analysis
2. Setting goals and priorities
3. Selection and development of people
4. Shaping the structure of the organization
5. Negotiating and consensus-building skills
6. Generating and introducing innovation

nization, and its major changes, may be described in extended statistical terms, citing demography, including educational levels, language, regional and age distribution, the technological factors, budgetary outlook, and the domestic and international competitive developments impinging on the institution. In most large-scale organizations such formal environmental analysis has come to be the starting point of strategic planning. At other times in other fields, the perception of environmental change is little more than the intuitive sensitivities of the leadership scanning the horizon with a finger to test the wind and steering by the seat of the pants. Such archaic methods have on occasion proved highly successful. Whatever the approach, executives across each of these four fields, in their numerous permutations, have the responsibility and function of perceiving and explaining the changing larger environment and specifying its impact on the organization.

Setting Goals and Priorities

The articulation of specific objectives and the establishment of priorities for an organization is a central feature of the executive common to these four organizations and, indeed, to almost any other executive worthy of the name. But the function is not simple. There may be competing objectives, and the achievement of one goal may diminish the possibility of accomplishing another. Resources of all kinds, including the time and energy of the executive, are limited. Moreover, the specification of goals and priorities may provoke keen internal conflict among factions and elements of the organization. The maintenance of a measure of internal cohesion and morale is vital to the mobilization of organizational effort and achievement of defined goals. All this is a fine art, for any organization trying to go several different ways at once or consumed in intensive conflict is not likely to go far.

Selection and Development of People

The central importance of human resources is common to these four organizations. All depend crucially on the performance of their people. But people do not come ready made as pegs to fit into fixed organizational holes. They need to be selected and recruited, trained, educated, moved about, promoted, motivated, compensated and rewarded, and even disciplined. The organization may even need to be reshaped on occasion to accommodate particular individuals and talents. The selection and development of people is at the center of the functions of the executive and the performance of the organization.

Shaping the Structure of the Organization

The molding and reshaping of the organization, in the light of the changing environment, the specified short-term and longer-term goals and priorities, and the development of its people is no less a distinctive function of the executive in these fields. The levels of the management hierarchy, the lines of reporting formally and informally, the controls over money flows, the relations with the press and media, relations to governments, and the interactions with other exterior groups are all reflective of the arrangement or structure of an organization. The executive is responsible for the contours and structure of the organization, although some features may be given by history and prove to be intractible for a period.

Negotiating and Consensus-Building Skills

In dealing with internal organizational problems, as well as external entities and constituencies, the skills of negotiation and consensus building are indispensable. Executives of these organizations are seldom able to achieve their objectives by simple fiat. Making allowance for differences in personal style, an organization seldom operates merely by the lines of formal authority, and external relations are seldom determined solely by impersonal markets or economic power.

Generating and Introducing Innovation

Change is typically mandated by different goals of the organization or the emerging environment. Executives are thus peculiarly concerned with the development and introduction of innovation. Change is inevitably a disturbance to an organization, or to some of its members, and inertia and resistance may thwart desired innovation or extract too high a cost in friction and conflict. The art of planning and introducing organizational change is a key feature of the job of the executive, more important in some organizations and at some periods than in others.

Distinctive Elements among Executives in Four Fields

Although the characteristics of executives in these fields in an important sense constitute an overlapping continuum, it is also instructive to identify the distinctive elements that characterize executives in each of these four fields (table 2–2). Although a modest degree of abstraction is necessarily involved, additional insights and generality are achieved.

Table 2–2
Contrasts among Four Fields

Element	Business	Government	Academic	Union
Measures of performance	Profits or value creation	Votes programs	Judgment of students, faculty, and alumni	Votes of members
Efficiency and equity	Market performance, efficiency	Largely equity	Academic efficiency bows to equity and custom	Largely internal equity
Command and persuasion	Command and control	Extensive persuasion first	Extensive and lengthy consultation	Administrative command and political notification on policy
Private or public processes	Private until released	Public at each step	Largely private with periodic exposure	Internal, officially controlled with informal lines
Personal constraints	Large degrees of management freedom	Strict civil service restraints and political process	Academic strict processes	Relative freedom except as limited by political and election processes
Length of service and time perspective	Relatively long term in most cases but with increasing insecurity	Limited by short-term election results	Relatively unconstrained although reduced in 1960s and 1970s	Renewed specified terms at national levels

Measures of Performance

The performance of the business executive is measured by the bottom line, short term or longer run, or by more sophisticated indicators of value creation in a market. Government executives are ultimately adjudged by the bottom line of impact on votes and by more diffused judgments of programmatic records, with few common denominators. The performance of academic executives tends to be related to the diffuse judgments and standards of the constituencies of students, faculty, and alumni. The performance of labor leaders is reflected in the perceived quality of the collective bargaining agreements they negotiate under the circumstances and the internal governance of the union expressed in votes of members or delegates at the next election largely in a one-party government. These are quite different substantive tests in quite different organizational settings.

Considerations of Efficiency and Equity

Markets subject business executives to the prime considerations of profits, productivity, and market performance while political executives, including senior civil servants, are far more concerned with relative equity and the appearance of fairness. Despite the rhetoric, to reshape a government to conform to an executive's view of efficiency is inhibited by the checks of the legislative and judicial branches. In the dimension of efficiency-equity, the academic executive confronts still different tests of efficiency, such as academic distinction and the number and quality of applications that cannot be ignored, but in general the trade-off leans toward custom and equity. Only extreme circumstances are likely to lead, for instance, to the closing of a department or a school on grounds of efficiency, and a layoff of tenured faculty on efficiency grounds is virtually unknown. In labor organizations the internal politics and the public law—the duty of fair representation—place the emphasis on the equity end of the efficiency-equity spectrum.

Command and Persuasion

The business executive achieves internal results—organizational structure, delegation, policy, and administration—by command and control. Orders are issued, incentives are provided, reports are received, and compliance is achieved or discipline dispensed as in a military-type organization. The governmental executive is far more indirect, probing the reactions of the wide array of constituencies in and out of government typically affected and the possible reactions of other branches of government, and paying great attention to the packaging and timing of proposals—in short, to the arts of persuasion rather than to the issuance of orders. The academic executive confronts endless consultation and debate in a milieu in which changing one's mind may be regarded as a virtue and in which various constituencies may assert overlapping claims of superiority. Union executives exert considerable control over internal administrative matters but typically require majority assent of membership on collective bargaining agreements, changes in the structure of the organization, and politically sensitive activities. Taking actions the executive is convinced are necessary for the organization—but are unpopular—often tests to the limits the powers of persuasion or the willingness occasionally to use up political capital.

Private or Public Processes

The processes of internal business decisions take place essentially in private and are made public or their consequences become evident at the discretion of the enterprise, although the timing of some reports may be dictated by government regulation. Indeed, there may even be government penalties for acting on insider information. In marked contrast, public executives, particularly in politically sensitive positions, are typically engaged in an exchange with press and the media at each step of the decision-making process. The news leak is well understood to be often a means of internal government conflict rather than the result of assiduous investigation by the news media. As Secretary of State George P. Shultz said, "We should recognize what life is like in Washington. The Canadian Ambassador coined the phrase, 'It's never over.' Nothing ever gets settled in this town. It's not like running a company or even a university. It's a seething debating society in which the debate never stops, in which people never give up, including me."[1] Academic executives usually have some of the freedom of business decision makers save that student newspapers often hound the process and academic participants are seldom constrained to express their views on pending matters as are members of management. Labor organization processes are seldom reported in the public press; the internal news organs ordinarily are in control of the leadership. Informal lines of internal communication often provide effective exchanges.

Personnel Constraints

The business executive has rather wide discretion in decisions on selection from within or drawing from outside the management organization and on assigning and compensating the management members of the organization. Any related reform or realignment of the management structure is no less pliable. There are, of course, some constraints established in public law, such as those related to race, sex, and age discrimination in personnel matters. Government executives, in contrast, face severe constraints by civil service rules, collective bargaining procedures, or requirements for political appointment. Recruitment procedures constrict choice, transfers and promotions are regulated, compensation is strictly confined, and discipline and discharge are subjected to complex and slow-moving procedures and appeals. I once compared the tasks of the government executive to the management of a glacier. The management of the professoriate in the academic world is no less constrained in process than the civil service, but personnel constraints applicable to executives outside the professoriate in private educational institutions are relatively unrestrained while in public institutions they are akin to higher levels of the civil service and the political processes. Labor union executives have relative freedom of appointment to staff save for the traditions of drawing from the ranks rather than from outsiders for line positions and as restricted by political considerations and assignment of certain posts to election results, as in the case of organizers or district directors in some unions.

Length of Service

This dimension of an organization affects the time horizon of an executive, as well as the turnover of executives, and may influence the stability of the organization. Business executives tend to have a considerable length of service, although they may be removed by the board of directors or top management. In recent years merger and takeover developments have placed these positions in some jeopardy, although many positions have been protected by various types of parachutes. The government executive is constrained by the calendar of elections, which bring changes not only among political appointees but rearrangements that affect the status of senior civil servants. This environment reinforces a short-term time horizon. Academic executives tend to serve for terms also without specification, although the late 1960s and 1970s saw a reduction in length of service. Elected officers of national unions tend to serve for specified terms of four or five years that tend to be renewed for relatively long periods, although there is much more turnover among elected local officials.

Changing Characteristics of Executives in Four Fields

Executives have been changing in these fields in part because of changes in their environment, in part because of developments in their organizations, and some of the change is attributable to the qualities of the executives, although it is not possible to assign magnitudes to these components of change.

Education

The general level of education in the United States, and the fraction with college degrees and professional training, continues to increase, affecting each generation of executives. Moreover, the past quarter-century has seen a rapid expansion in the extent of executive education—short courses, often at universities, designed for practicing executives to meet with similar executives from other organizations for periods such as four to twelve weeks to consider issues confronting decision makers portrayed in cases, to be instructed on recent developments and new techniques, and to reflect on organizational processes and goals. These programs have become widespread for executives drawn from business and government and are probably less extensive for academic and trade union executives. Harvard University's Graduate School of Business Administration began its Advanced Management Program after World War II, a variety of programs in its School of Government date from the 1970s, programs for higher education executives date from the 1960s, and the Trade Union Program was established in 1942.

But it is easy to exaggerate the influence of formal education in the development of executives: "Since fewer than 20 percent of the chief executive officers of large corporations have business school degrees (although the figure is rising), there is even a nagging possibility that formal training is unnecessary for effective management."[2] Given the extraordinary range of work performed by federal government employees, it is not surprising that their executives are not well trained throughout the service.[3] Academic executives in the major positions are seldom selected primarily for their managerial skills or executive training, and labor union leaders are elected in a process that is not likely to stress executive skills either.

Promoting and Entry from Outside

The ladders of promotion and the ports of entry to executive positions in these organizations help to shape the executive. It is vital also to inquire whether there have been any significant changes in these routes to executive posts in recent years. In business organizations internal promotion is the most common route to general managerial and executive posts. But the transfer from other organizations, particularly other businesses, has been made more frequent in recent years by the willingness of enterprises to look outside combined with the growth of personnel recruitment firms, or head hunters, as a serious business undertaking, as well as by the merger and takeover processes that reshuffle executives.

In the government service, the civil service provides various, though limited, points of entry and ladders of promotions. That system has not reflected significant change in recent years despite the creation of the senior civil service and the effort to encourage greater mobility. Political appointees constitute the other entry and structure of advancement for executives, and here again there appears to have been little change, although the proportion of posts that are political appointees has been much increased in recent years.

Most academic executives, as might be expected, come directly out of academic or administrative life on a college campus. As high as 85 percent of presidents come from this source, and half of the remainder have had experience in academic life as a faculty member or administrator. "This route of access is natural because academic institutions have their own ways of

doing things and it is important to be acquainted intimately with them."[4]
Most academic presidents (80 percent), however, come directly from outside
the institution they become chief executive. Length of service has declined
from ten to twelve years prior to the mid-1960s to seven years currently.

National union executives are selected almost without exception from
their members and ordinarily by the well-defined ladder consisting of business manager of a local union, a representative for the national union, a vice-
president of the national union, and the top office. There may be some vari-
ation in the steps in the ladder, including another local union office, an officer
of a district council, joint board, or some other intermediate body, or health
and welfare or pension fund administrator. Only extremely rarely does an
outsider, a non-rank-and-file member, reach the top through a professional
staff role. C. Wright Mills wrote in 1948, "The union world is a world of
political machines; the labor leader is a machine politician."[5] Only a deadlock
between communist and noncommunist factions brought Ralph Helstein, the
union's lawyer, as a compromise candidate to the presidency of the Packing-
house Workers after World War I. Unlike some unions in other countries,
political leaders, newspaper editors, or leaders of social movements are not
likely to enter the leadership of American labor unions. The public regulation
of the election process in U.S. unions by the Labor-Management Reporting
and Disclosure Act of 1959 (Title IV) has not made significant changes in
ports of entry or internal ladders to executive posts.

Executives and Constituents

The relationship between executives (leaders) and lower-level officers of the
organization and the main body of constituents is vital to the performance of
the organization and to ways it may have changed over a period of years.
There are, of course, marked differences generally between the interactions
of business executives and stockholders; government executives and legislative bodies and voters; academic executives and the constituents of students,
faculty, and alumni or legislators; and union executives and members. Each
setting is surrounded by internal rivalries or opposition and by the relevant
press and media. Moreover, the relationships also vary according to whether
the organization is in a period of calm or crisis, prosperity or recession, or
rapid growth or stagnation.

"One generalization that is supported by research and experience is that
effective two-way communication is essential to the proper functioning of the
leader-follower relationship."[6] It needs to be borne in mind that few organizations or constituencies are homogeneous and that executives are ever at
work in two-way processes, in some organizations more than others, to develop a full consensus or a working consent to policies and administration.
Line executives in business have historically been less involved in this process
since it was deemed less necessary, although recent years have seen vastly

more attention to stockholder communications and the courting of major shareholders and stock analysts.

Executives in all four fields in recent years have been confronted with new problems that probably require new methods in their relationships to lower-level officials and constituencies. The stockholders, electorates, and memberships have become better educated and more widely read, and much more information or disinformation is available almost instantly. The television medium, which cannot be fully influenced, has direct access to the constituency. As a consequence, these constituencies have become in many cases more independent and more divided or less homogeneous in their willingness to follow the executive blindly. Such constituents are more vulnerable to external as well as internal opposition. The executives in many cases have been compelled to devote much more time and energy to the reinforcement of the organization and to systematic discourse and education of lower levels of the organization and to constituents. "A loyal constituency is won when people, consciously or unconsciously, judge the leader to be capable of solving their problems and meeting their needs, when the leader is seen as symbolizing their norms, and then their image of the leader (whether or not it corresponds with reality) is congruent with their inner environment of myth and legend."[7]

The tasks of executives are often made more difficult by these modern conditions, particularly when rapid and major changes are dictated by the environmental analysis and the goals of the organization. The constituencies are more independent, more divided, less willing to accept the dictates of the executive, and more likely to mount demonstrations and opposition.

New executive methods and styles are generated, and new types of executives are called. Business executives need to be at home in dealing with government officials, legislators, international constituents, and the media, as well with finance, production, and marketing. Government executives require even more developed skills of accommodation and sensitivity to constituencies. "Academic executives are many-faced, in the sense that they must face in many directions at once while contriving to turn one's back on no important group. . . . They are mostly a mediator."[8] Union executives need to accommodate their membership, employers with whom their organization deals, governmental agencies, and the public. The task of generating organizational momentum toward cherished goals is constrained by managing diverse internal elements and external constituencies. There is little room between destructive organizational conflict and immobility in a rapidly changing environment.

Generational Changes

The generational contrasts between those who grew up with experience in the Great Depression and World War II and those who reached maturity in the 1970s and 1980s are said to have significant impacts on all of these four fields, on both executives and their constituencies. These age contrasts affect the characteristics of constituents and affect in significant ways the performance of executives and the methods they use to achieve organizational goals.

Surveys suggest that these generational contrasts are not influenced by ethnic background, occupation, or sector of the economy.

- The older generation, products of the World War II era, accept authority. The younger generation, having grown up during Vietnam, do not trust authority.
- The older generation see work as a duty, an instrument through which they can support themselves and their families. The younger generation believe work should be fun, a social occasion.
- The older generation believe experience is the necessary road to promotion, and are willing to spend time in "apprenticeship." The younger generation see no reason to wait, believing people should advance just as quickly as their competence permits.
- The older generation believe in tact. The younger generation demands honesty and candor—to them, tact is seen as evasion of the issues.
- The older generation believe that fairness is achieved by treating everyone the same. The younger generation believe that fairness requires that individuals should be allowed to be different."

These characteristics of the younger generation suggest the need for "a better fit between a company and the individuals who compose it; we need a lively, open, risk-taking view of the world in corporations today."[9]

The postwar baby boom was such a large cohort in the population as it moved through the educational system and out into the world of work that it is not entirely surprising that its distinctive values and aspirations have affected these four organizations and the way they operate. The rapid growth of women and minorities in executive positions constitutes another set of new influences. But organizations and their traditions are great disciplinarians over a lifetime, and it is uncertain how much and in which directions the new generation or the organizations will eventually change. At best they are likely to be subtle. The influence of this new generation is introduced gradually, not as a sudden revolution as with the Lenin revolution or workers-management in Yugoslavia.

Some Degree of Convergence

The developments and their consequences recounted above have some disproportional impacts on the four types of organizations and their executives, but in general they also seem to be making the roles of executives somewhat more similar, or reducing their variance. For business enterprises these developments are particularly relevant to politically salient industries and larger enterprises in which executives have neither the unilateral authority nor unique competence to set policies on account of the diverse constituencies with which they must negotiate, often including governments.[10] Such industries are widespread, particularly in a more competitive international setting, and in an economy in which government so directly impinges on business, as in such sectors as automobiles, semiconductors, airframe, textiles, agribusiness, and health care. In such settings executives are less and less able alone to follow the textbook of business strategic planning and decision making. They are dependent on their negotiations with the U.S. government over a wide range of questions, including environmental standards and local taxes and subsidies, with foreign governments over overseas facilities, with labor organizations, and with financial institutions. In other ways, some business executives must deal with boycotts and other public demonstrations aroused by concern with investments in South Africa, by environmental advocacy, or by the conditions of migrants on farms supplying produce, such as Campbell Soup Company. In these circumstances business executives appear less traditionally businesslike and reflect some affinity to the executives of government, academic institutions, and labor organizations. It is appropriate that the education of business executives include more attention to these newer problems and involve more interaction with elements common to the training of executives in these other fields.[11]

One of the factors contributing to a degree of convergence among executives is the systematic development of multicareers particularly between the private sector (business, academia, or labor organizations) and government. When the same individual has had executive responsibility in several fields, there is a likelihood, although no certainty, that there may be less absolutism in the dealing among these organizations and more understanding of their internal processes and decision making.[12] There are substantial impediments—financial, legal, educational, and cultural—to dual careers in the public and private sectors, but there can be substantial benefits, as Sol Linowitz urges:

> I believe it would serve both the nation and the enterprise community if more people in the private sector spent some part of their careers in government service. A business man who has worked for the government and brings his understanding of that world back to the private sector makes a real contribution to his company. And while serving the government he can make a special contribution to his country, provided that he has moved into a different national sub-culture with different purposes.[13]

There has long been some exchange between academic careers and government, and wartimes have expanded this exchange, as it has with the business executive community. An early experience in the World War I period was that of Frank W. Taussig, a Harvard economist, on the Tariff Commission and the Price-Fixing Committee of the War Industries Board. The New Deal and World War II initiated a broad flow. The first Ph.D. to serve in the cabinet was Postmaster John A. Gronowski under President Johnson (1963–1965), and in my period (1975) there were five in the cabinet.

Among labor leaders there have been far fewer appointments to executive posts in national government for a variety of reasons. A notable exception in this generation is Thomas R. Donahue, now secretary-treasurer of the AFL-CIO, who served as an assistant secretary of the Department of Labor in the 1960s. This experience well served the government and contributed significantly to the development of a ranking labor executive. A greater exchange of able talent from private sectors with government is vital to the development of effective public administration in a democratic society.

A comment needs to be made about executives of business trade associations, academic associations, and labor union federations as compared to executives in the constituent organization within each field. The standard type of organization in each field is different from the confederation level. The executives of the Chamber of Commerce, the National Association of Manufacturers, the Association of State Legislators, the American Association of Universities, or the AFL-CIO have less freedom of decision than most of the constituent organizations on many issues that would affect the constituent members. Thus they tend to behave even more as mediators than the executives of affiliated organizations, who are ordinarily free to leave the confederation at will. Moreover, many distinguished executives of constituent organizations do poorly as leaders of confederations. For instance, John L. Lewis and Walter Reuther were great leaders of national unions but not so effective as executives of confederations. The functions and skills of the two levels of governance are quite different.

Notes

1. *New York Times,* December 9, 1986, p. A-14.

2. Derek Bok, *Higher Learning* (Cambridge: Harvard University Press, 1986), p. 104.

3. Howard Rosen, *Servants of the People: The Uncertain Future of the Federal Civil Service* (Salt Lake City: Olympus Publishing Company, 1985).

4. Clark Kerr and Marian L. Jade, *The Many Lives of Academic Presidents: Time, Place and Character* (Washington, D.C.: Association of Governing Boards of Universities and Colleges, 1986), pp. 18–19.

5. C. Wright Mills, *The New Men of Power: America's Labor Leaders* (New York: Harcourt Brace and Company, 1948), p. 5.

6. John W. Gardner, *The Heart of the Matter: Leader-Constituent Interaction*, Leadership Papers, No. 3 (Washington, D.C.: Independent Sector, 1986), p. 9.

7. Ibid., p. 11.

8. Clark Kerr, *The Uses of the University* (Cambridge: Harvard University Press, 1963), pp. 29, 36.

9. D.Q. Mills in Bureau of National Affairs, *Daily Labor Report*, September 10, 1986, p. A-4. For a full discussion, see D. Quinn Mills, *Not Like Our Parents: How the Baby Boom Generation Is Changing America* (New York: Morrow, 1987).

10. Malcolm S. Salter, "Industrial Governance and Corporate Performance, research project (Boston: Harvard Business School, May 1985).

11. John T. Dunlop, ed., *Business and Public Policy* (Cambridge: Harvard University Press, 1980).

12. *American Society, Public and Private Responsibilities*, ed. Winthrop Knowlton and Richard Zeckhauser (Cambridge, Mass.: Ballinger, 1986).

13. Sol Linowitz, *The Making of a Public Man* (Boston: Little, Brown, 1985), p. 241.

3
Strategic Planning in Labor Organizations

T here are common roles, as well as distinctive elements, in the functions of executives in different types of organizations. The shared activities include environmental assessment, setting goals and priorities, the shaping of the structure of an organization and its operations, the selection and development of people, and the introduction of innovation and change. These five common elements of the responsibility of executives in bodies of some scale and continuity may be distilled into the process of strategic planning.

The concept of strategic planning as just defined for organizations in general is consistent with the classic formulation of corporate planning and strategy by Kenneth R. Andrews:

> Corporate strategy is the pattern of decisions in a company that determines and reveals its objectives, purposes and goals, produces the principal policies and plans for achieving those goals, and defines the range of businesses the company is to pursue, the kind of economic and human organization it is or intends to be, and the nature of the economic and non-economic contribution it intends to make to its shareholders, employees, customers and communities.[1]

In one sense, the principles involved in strategic planning and its processes are little more than the common sense that leaders of most organizations, including unions, develop and apply intuitively and as a matter of practicality. On the other hand, there has been considerable resistance to such approaches as importing inapplicable business methods and being insensitive to the inherent political processes and democratic procedures that characterize governments and unions.

Democratic processes and standards may well interfere with the pure efficiency of the economy or an organization, but it is surely inappropriate to argue that good management, including the basic elements of strategic planning, is irrelevant to governmental agencies or labor organizations.[2]

Fortunately it is not necessary to argue over the applicability of strategic planning to labor organizations as a matter of principle or ideology, for a limited number of labor organizations have instituted such processes in their organizations, produced reports on their future goals, directions, plans, and structure, and established mechanisms to implement such plans. This chapter examines several of these cases in detail—those of the Communication Workers of America and the International Union of Bricklayers and Allied Craftsmen—that involve strategic planning and others that adopt an element of strategic planning. Moreover, other national unions have begun the full process; for example, the United Automobile Workers has set up the Commission on the Future.

The scope of some of these plans has been broad, encompassing all five of the elements noted above, while others have been narrower, concerned primarily, for instance, with the structure of the organization. But issues of structure necessarily involve questions of environmental analysis, goals, and priorities.

One observation that emerges from the reports and activities of labor organizations that have undertaken a systematic review of their environment and a planning effort, with their staff and members alone or with the assistance of outside consultants, has been that the process itself has been highly rewarding. The by-products in insights and new approaches have changed many views of the environment, the organization, and the perceived views of some members. These new perspectives have been no less of interest than the formal report and plan that emerged.

Notes

1. Kenneth R. Andrews, *The Concept of Corporate Strategy* (Homewood, Ill.: Irwin, 1980), p. 18; 3d ed. (1987), p. 13.
2. Derek C. Bok and John T. Dunlop, *Labor and the American Community* (New York: Simon and Schuster, 1970), pp. 139–140.

CASE 1

COMMUNICATIONS WORKERS OF AMERICA,
COMMITTEE ON THE FUTURE

The Communication Workers of America (CWA) was established in 1947, replacing the National Federation of Telephone Workers founded in 1938.[1] In 1949 the CWA affiliated with the CIO.

As President Glenn E. Watts stated, from its outset the union has been confronted by change: "Change in power centers and changes in external and internal influence. From the typewriter to the word processor; from hot lead to fiber optics; and from mechanization to automation, we have lived through change into today's high-tech Information Age."[2] The union has had a history in this environment of periodic review of policy and structure, such as with the 1971 structure review committee.

The Committee on the Future was created in June 1981 by convention action, at the suggestion of local unions in District 9. The report of the committee, in excess of 200 pages, was presented to a special convention in March 1983.[3]

The committee was instructed by the 1981 convention to "look at our total environment and at ourselves." It thus defined its mission in this way:

> Analyze strategic options open to the Union for dealing in a positive way with important changes taking place in our environment.
>
> Draw upon ideas of the Union membership, officers and staff.
>
> Examine areas both inside and outside the Union.
>
> Present strategic recommendations and present a plan for structural changes if any were necessary.
>
> Adhere to the basic purpose of strengthening and enlarging CWA, making it a more meaningful and effective force in serving the interests of our members, now and in the future.

The Committee on the Future had fourteen members, one elected from each of the CWA's twelve districts, one representing public workers, and the president as chairman. The CWA's executive board called the committee "the movement's first experiment in long-range strategic planning." In the course of the committee's work in January 1982, the breakup of ATT was announced, an event that had significant effects on the communications industry and the CWA.

The committee engaged in a systematic process of research, gathering extensive technical and statistical information and interviewing at least seven experts drawn from labor, business, technological areas, and academia.[4] It developed a scenario of the future that it tested widely with union officers and members. It used the idea of a successful information age union as a basis for specific recommendations after factoring in suggestions and ideas from a cross-section of the union. An interim report was reviewed by the delegates to the 1982 union's convention.

The committee then refined its recommendations for new CWA initiatives in bargaining, organizing, and political and legislative action, and it considered changes needed in union structure, funding, and ways of operating to support the recommended new initiatives currently and over the longer future.

The following excerpts from the Committee on the Future report provide more detail as to its methods and recommendations:

Summary

What stands out with absolute clarity is that the challenge to CWA over the coming decade is above all to provide our present and future Members with employment security. There is no other Union goal of greater importance or wider application than this one, which touches all of our lives and reaches into the heart of all our hopes.

The key to employment security is through training and retraining, so that we can ride the crest of the wave of technological change. To do this we must be able to gain access to the funds of employers and government, for we cannot do the job alone. While we cannot lay aside our powerful confrontational skills, there is no way we can achieve employment security through training and retraining if we and our employers get bogged down in the old ways. Careful new initiatives in bargaining, political action, joint consultation, and public relations will be necessary.

The Committee calls the attention of the membership to a number of external forces and conditions that, in our view, make it absolutely essential that CWA equip itself to operate as a strategy-driven Union. We cannot afford to deal with external events reactively and in a piecemeal way.

The forces to which we refer include (a) major technological change that will profoundly affect our job opportunities; (b) structural changes in the telecommunications/data processing industry; (c) changes in the composition, lifestyles, needs, and interests of the workforce; (d) power shifts in business and politics; and (e) economic turbulence and uncertainty.

The Committee sees these external forces both as threatening, if we fail to deal with them, and as great opportunities, if we rise to the occasion. Unlike some unions, we are favorably positioned to ride with the forces of the future.

To get ourselves ready to meet this challenge, we found much to be done inside our Union. The Committee looked at every aspect of CWA's activities for the purpose of finding out how we could best use each one to reinforce an overall, integrated strategy, never losing sight of the guiding purpose—the achievement of employment security for our Members.

What this situation calls for is nothing less than the "renewal" of our Union. These efforts at renewal must be carefully planned, and the plan must be so well put together and executed as to be more powerful as a whole than the sum of its separate parts.

To carry out such a plan successfully, all of us in CWA will have to learn more effective ways to play our roles. We will have to tighten our financial and budgetary controls. We will have to generate internal savings through greater efficiency. We will have to free up resources for new programs by better management of our Staff. We will have to achieve higher rates of growth and higher degrees of effective performance at all levels. And we will have to persist in our efforts to improve the well being of women and minorities.

As we bargain and lobby for greater employment security, we must be flexible enough to track with rapidly shifting external power centers and strong enough in state and national politics to help get America back on a sounder social and economic foundation.

There is probably no Member or group of Members in the CWA family who will not feel some internal jolts and disturbances as a result of the changes in Union processes and procedures that we will need to make. But we can take this, because the prize—employment security—is worth it. And because the alternative is to watch thousands of our Members become victims of America's move into the Information Age and the global economy.

Ten years from now—even five years from now—when we look back on the CWA of 1983, we may hardly recognize what we now find so familiar and comfortable. But we will be looking back from a strong and secure position made possible by the fact that we saw the need in time, we developed a strategy in time, and we began moving in time. . . .

The Committee on the Future's Base Scenario

We believe that our society is in the process of undergoing some fundamental and far-reaching changes. The basic cause for these changes is the fact that the Industrial Age is on the way out. Two hundred years ago, when machines were added to muscle power, the Agricultural Age gave way to the Industrial Revolution. Now the Industrial Age is giving way to an Age of Information in which microprocessors are being linked to brain power. Twenty years from now, less than 20 percent of the U.S. workforce may handle all of our production in highly automated factories. In agriculture today, only two percent of our workforce feeds 220 million Americans, with food left over for export.

The Coming of the Information Era

As the Industrial Age fades, the U.S. economy of the 1980s will be marked by periods of inflation and unemployment and an erratic pattern of economic growth. The U.S. will become less and less self-sufficient and will be pulled into a very complex and competitive global economy.

In fact, the Information (and Service) Age has already started. In 1957 for the first time, more people were employed in the information part of the U.S. economy than in the declining industrial sector. In 1978, those employed in the service sector of the U.S. economy exceeded those working in the industrial portion. We are headed toward a "wired society." People at home and work will be increasingly interconnected and able to interact and exchange information through communications and data networks.

Transitional Turbulence

In the next 20 to 30 years of transition from the Industrial to the Information Age, there will be serious disruptions and dislocations in the U.S. workforce. Already, we are seeing the early stages of decline of such basic U.S. industries, as steel, rubber, and automobiles. The textile and shoe industries have already declined considerably. Foreign manufacturers are becoming dominant in these industries, and many U.S. jobs will disappear.

Along with the decline of these traditional industries, an increasing amount of industrial work will be taken over by robots. The robot factory is almost here.

As a result of such changes, workers will place stronger emphasis on employment security, career development, training and retraining, and support for job relocation.

Transition to the Information Age will also bring other kinds of continuous and rapid changes. Through the use of computers, different parts of the telecommunications/information industry are becoming interconnected. AT&T, IBM, the Postal Service, and many other organizations are rapidly becoming part of one huge, expanding combination of interrelated businesses. The use of electronic work stations and local, regional, and international data and communication networks is spreading rapidly. By 1990, today's four million work stations will grow to 25 to 30 million.

Changing Work Patterns

Working patterns by 2000 will be very different from what they are today. Information Age technology will permit many tasks to be done both at home and in widely dispersed work locations. Other activities will be done in a central location. The Information Age could also increase threats to personal liberties and privacy. A society monitored and manipulated by "big brother's" information technology, as described in George Orwell's novel, *1984,* could become a reality.

As the Information Age becomes established, workers and their jobs will be affected dramatically. New careers will open up with new kinds of jobs. These will call for more knowledge and decisionmaking, requiring more training and retraining. Rigidly defined jobs are on the way out. With a growing economy, the number of jobs will greatly increase. In the longer term, many more job and career opportunities will be created because new information systems will have to be designed, installed, and maintained while others are reconfigured.

Career-minded workers are likely to be more committed to their own interests than to those of their employers. They will want to acquire "portable skills" that they can take with them from employer to employer. In the transitional period, some workers will be displaced by technology and foreign competition. They will need retraining to adapt to the new jobs of the Information Age.

The white-collar portion of the workforce will continue to expand and change its characteristics. In the Information Age, white-collar workers will have more to do with identifying and solving problems and less to do as cogs in a clerical machine. Distinctions in both job content and status between white-collar workers, supervisors, and management will become blurred. White-collar working conditions will change to meet specific local needs. White-collar workers especially will be highly mobile, well-educated, and concerned primarily with their own needs. They are unlikely to be loyal to a single employer for long periods of time.

A Changing Workforce

As we move further into the Information Age, the composition and the attitudes of the workforce will change significantly. Women, older workers, and part-timers will form larger portions of the workforce. Workers will want the right to have higher-level decisions explained and justified and the right to make inputs to them. They will also insist on being treated with dignity and will be increasingly concerned with the quality of their life in the workplace. They will want more opportunities to influence their working conditions.

All these changes will result in much less uniformity in workers' needs and interests. There will probably be a greater desire for the ability to select job benefits based on individual needs ("cafeteria benefits"). Nevertheless, workers will continue to feel entitled to more and more.

Changes in Management Behavior

Overall, we believe that *traditional* unionism will have considerably less appeal to Information Age workers than it has had to workers of the Industrial Age. The Information Age will also affect management behavior. Management will increase its efforts both to avoid unionization and to weaken the appeal and effectiveness of unions. Management will place heavy emphasis on cost reduction and productivity improvement. They will use arguments about foreign competition to increase pressure on unions to hold down wages and win concessions.

The "scientific" management techniques introduced by Frederick Taylor for the Industrial Age are being replaced in some companies. The new management style is less controlling, less rigid and authoritarian, and more in tune with the requirements of information technology. Also, management will put a premium on creative employees, giving them more appreciation, encouragement, and rewards than before.

Management will argue that unions are unnecessary and counterproductive. Together with anti-union government, they will push for policies opposed to traditional unions. Some will try to use management-controlled employee participation schemes—without any real transfer of power—to lessen unions' clout or to prove that their employees don't need a union. They will try to avoid unionization by appealing to the new needs and interests of workers.

Lower-level supervisors will be squeezed in pay and promotion opportunities between two forces. From below, there will be pressures due to the rising responsibility levels of white-collar workers. From above, there will be pressures caused by fewer promotions to higher-level jobs because these jobs will continue to be occupied by members of the 40-year-old population bulge (a consequence of the post World War II baby boom). The old basis of supervisor's authority—their broader job knowledge and their enforcement of work rules—will begin to crumble.

Impact on Unions

We believe that the Information Age will affect labor unions' organizing and bargaining efforts. Growth of the labor movement will depend on whether and how unions adapt to changes in the workforce, changes in workers' needs and interests, and changes in management and government strategies. While the growing ranks of white-collar workers could benefit from union representation, unions right now do not appeal to many of them. The unions' present image and power base is tied to the declining blue-collar industrial portion of the economy.

Unions will need to develop new strategies based on changes in the workforce and in workers' skills and attitudes. Supervisors will be increasingly ripe for unionization as their frustration level rises. The anti-union attitudes of the 1980s will require renewed emphasis on labor's political action activities.

In the interest of their members, some unions may be encouraged to try to get more involved in how company policies and strategies get set—rather than reacting to management decisions after the fact. For example, plant locations and shutdowns, mergers, scope of QWL [quality of work life], and product pricing are the kinds of decisions unions will want to influence. A U.S. version of the German policy of required worker representation on company boards of directors ("co-determination") could emerge.

As the Information Age develops, an increasing amount of local negotiating is apt to occur on the job on a nearly continuous basis. Problem-solving, flexible job definitions and hours, and stronger participation in decision-making are items that workers will want to negotiate frequently at the local level.

As the Industrial Age declines, the economic gap between "haves" and "have-nots" within the total U.S. working population will widen. As some jobs disappear and others are downgraded, and as public assistance to the disadvantaged is cut back, the condition of the have-nots will become steadily worse. Alienated have-nots and minorities may form and join new types of associations or "unions" in an attempt to solve their problems.

Within the organized part of the workforce, the gap between strong, affluent unions and weak, poor unions will widen, distorting income distribution. For example, unions in growth industries may win pension and other gains that can adversely affect the buying power of those union members in declining industries. We expect that single-industry unions will be a thing of the past. Just as plantwide and industrywide CIO unions met a need in the 1930s not met by AFL's single-craft unions, so tomorrow's big unions will spread across single-industry boundaries. In tomorrow's multiple-industry union, different strategies for different bargaining tables will be required. . . .

Summary of Recommendations

The elements of an integrated strategy for the future set forth above contain 19 specific recommendations for action here and now. Most of them are procedural and can be set in motion at once if this Convention approves.

Those having constitutional implications are recapped in the next and last part of this section of the report.

These recommendations will satisfy the demands of the present situation and will see us on our way. No doubt further changes will be necessary as the AT&T/BOC [Bell Operating Companies] reorganization plan unfolds and as the demands and opportunities of the Information Age come into sharper focus. It would, however, be premature to try to formulate these changes now; the new Strategic Planning and Budget Committee in its role as a planning body should make further recommendations as the need for them arises.

For the present, we believe that the most urgent matters are (1) forceful, integrated strategies for each CWA bargaining and growth sector that has a common set of interests; (2) stronger contract language and new bargaining agenda items to promote employment security; (3) a permanent planning unit linked to ways and means; (4) tighter financial and budgetary controls; (5) new sources of funds; (6) focused external growth; (7) stronger influence on state and national legislation; (8) better compliance with clear standards for Local and District performance; (9) improvement in Staff morale and effectiveness.

The full list of recommendations contained in this section of the report follows:

1. Establish CWA strategy centers, on a trial basis, to serve each of the Union's major objectives in the main areas of collective bargaining, external growth, and political/legislative action—all integrated around the ultimate goals of employment security for our Members.

2. Assign to the Strategic Planning and Budget Committee the combined powers and responsibilities of the existing Ways and Means Committee and of a strategic planning committee to make recommendations to the Executive Board; and instruct the President to supply the necessary staff support and coordination of inputs from headquarters departments.

3. In the interest of employment security, strengthen current contract language and pursue new bargaining agenda items.

4. Provide for an elected National Director, with a voice in Executive Board proceedings, to represent CWA's public worker Members.

5. Establish clear standards for performance for Locals, together with a self-review process to encourage and assist satisfactory compliance.

6. Establish clear standards for District performance, together with a self-review process to encourage and assist satisfactory compliance.

7. Establish an ad hoc charter review and clarification process.

8. Modify the rule on selection of delegates to ensure a proper representation at conventions.

9. Prohibit proxy voting at conventions.

10. Adopt a more professional approach to managing CWA Staff, working with them to upgrade their morale, motivation, and performance.

11. Explore, with caution, possible new approaches to conflict avoidance so that some of the excessive time and money spent on grievances can be put to other uses.

12. Move to a biennial Convention and to quadrennial election for national officers—and for Local officers when the law permits. Give high priority to getting the law changed.

13. Instruct the Security-Treasurer to prepare a comprehensive set of recommendations for tighter systems of financial and budgetary control for submission to the 1983 regular Convention.

14. Mandate State councils in all states in which CWA has a significant presence—modeled after the successful ones already in place.

15. Require CWA Locals to affiliate with state AFL-CIO bodies at a level and in a manner appropriate to their special circumstances.

16. Have CWA vigorously pursue a sophisticated and aggressive public relations program.

17. Create a fourth elective executive vice presidency with the hope and expectation of electing a woman to fill it. As a full-fledged member of the Executive Board, she would receive her assigned responsibilities from the President in the same manner as all other EVPs [executive vice-presidents].

18. Instruct the Executive Board to formulate specific constitutional definitions of associate membership and affiliation for Convention action, with a view to meeting the needs of retired Members, unemployed Members, and former Members now working in nonunion jobs.

19. Establish a Public Appeals Board composed of distinguished persons not otherwise associated with the Union as an additional recourse in all classes of internal disputes.

Constitutional Matters Arising from the Final Report of the Committee on the Future

Several of the 19 recommendations listed immediately above have constitutional implications. Notice of these eight having been given to the delegates to this Convention 60 days prior to its convening, they can be voted up or down by a simple majority. They are as follows:

1. Modification of standards for Locals by adding a requirement that Locals affiliate with state AFL-CIO bodies.
2. Modification of formula for selection of delegates to conventions.
3. Provision for biennial conventions.
4. Provision for quadrennial election of officers.
5. Provision for a Public Appeals Board.
6. Provision mandating State Councils.
7. Prohibition of proxy voting at conventions.
8. Provision for an elected National Director representing public workers.

Notes

1. Twentieth Century Fund, *How Collective Bargaining Works* (New York: Twentieth Century Fund, 1942), pp. 952–954; Joseph A. Beirne, *Challenge to Labor, New Roles for American Trade Unions* (Englewood Cliffs, N.J.: Prentice-Hall, 1969); Raymond Williams and Glenn Watts, "The Process of Working Together: CWA's/ATT's Approach to QWL" in *Teamwork—Joint Labor—Management Programs in America,* ed. Jerome M. Rosow (New York: Pergamon Press, 1986), pp. 75–88; John R. Meyer et al., *The Economics of Competition in the Telecommunications Industry* (Cambridge, Mass.: Oelgeschlager, Gunn and Hain, 1980).

2. See Communications Workers of America, *Committee on the Future Report* (Washington, D.C.: CWA, March 1983), p. 3.

3. All quotations that follow are drawn from ibid.: pp. 3, 7–8, 61–65, 54–56.

4. I testified before the committee.

CASE 2
BRICKLAYERS—PROJECT 2000

The International Union of Bricklayers and Allied Craftsmen (BAC) was founded in 1865 and is the oldest construction national union in North America.[1] As President John T. Joyce stated in establishing the Committee on the Year 2000 in February 1984, "Over the last 10 years . . . the two depressions we have gone through have resulted in the loss of one-third of our members" [from approximately 150,000]." Part of the decline was a consequence of losses in parts of the brick construction market and part a consequence of the growth in nonunion contractors and their share of the work. Moreover, an added concern arose from the judgment broadly believed that survival will require a membership of 200,000 to 250,000 if a union in the construction industry is to be able to be effective in the twenty-first century at a reasonable dues rate.

The assignment to the Project 2000 Committee, composed of twenty-nine business agents from the United States and Canada, was to develop "a blueprint to guide the Union over the next decade and a half." The charge was "to undertake a long-range planning effort, an organizational strategy."[2]

The committee met in a series of two-to-six-day conferences over a period of eighteen months. It took testimony from a broad range of union representatives, contractors, architects, engineers, academics,[3] and other experts—seventy-one in all. It gathered and studied extensive statistical data on shipments, construction, competing products, share or market, advertising, and regional developments. The future of various masonry markets was analyzed and projected, as was the role of changes in technology. It sought the views of the membership and arranged a number of opinion polls designed to secure the points of view of the members on a wide range of questions.

The committee organized its work into five major topics with a subcommittee assigned to each: developing the masonry industry, union administration and structure, membership services, membership growth, and relations with organizations outside masonry.

At least two conclusions developed in the course of the discussions helped to shape its recommendations: the union must take a leading role in the revitalization of the masonry industry, and the union is a service organization, by which it meant:

> Our members want us to help them gain well-paid employment and benefits that provide a sense of security, of course. But beyond these economic needs, they have concerns for the quality of work life and for fostering a spirit of mutual aid and fraternity among craftsmen.
>
> Members want to develop and use new skills to create products of high quality—they want their Union not only to guarantee rights of the workplace, but also to work with contractors and others to improve management and assure that it is fair, respectful, and effective. A new vision of the Union must address this central reality.

The summary of the recommendation of the Project 2000 Committee report, more than a hundred pages long, follows.[4]

Summary of Recommendations

General

BAC should continue to be a masonry-centered craft and allied worker union, concentrating its resources on masonry and holding to a broad view of what constitutes the masonry process in order to assure that its trade jurisdiction be protected and expanded. It should take all appropriate steps to assure that the employers of its members share this broad vision of masonry and support the Union's efforts to control for its members all work within this purview.

Masonry Industry Development

The fate of our Union is tied to the fortunes of the masonry industry in the United States and Canada. BAC, therefore, has an inescapable responsibility to exercise a position of industry leadership and use its resources to support programs that will advance the industry's interests. The Union should establish as a goal:

- The creation of a $20-million-per-year national/regional masonry advertising and promotion program in the U.S. and Canada. And that the IU [International Union] appoint a task force to work through IMI [International Masonry Institute] to develop a masonry warranty program.
- The creation of a $20-million-per-year masonry research and development program in our two countries.
- Full implementation of the National/Regional Trowel Trades Training System as soon as is practicable.
- Execution of these three programs through the International Masonry Institute.
- Funding of these programs by collectively-bargained contributions amounting to three percent of the basic wage/fringe benefits package (or about one half of one percent of the industry's revenues), and education of BAC members and the industry to approach such a funding method as the only proven way of masonry industry funding, and as the most equitable available means of spreading among all its beneficiaries legitimate industry business costs.

Beyond Masonry

Our Union must continue to develop and strengthen broad working relationships in the labor community in the U.S. and Canada and abroad, exert a positive influence on legislative and political affairs in the U.S. and Canada; join forces when it can with business and other groups who share our objectives and philosophy; and educate and inform clients of the building industry, and the general public, about the values and activities of our Union and the advantages of masonry construction.

Collective Bargaining

BAC must study and consider instituting all programmatic and structural changes in collective bargaining that will extend the process to all parts of the masonry industry, help assure that the process provides our members with adequate wages, benefits and working conditions, provides the broadest possible support for masonry industry development programs, and affords the greatest possible opportunities for our members and Union to participate in strategic decision-making processes in the masonry industry. The Union should further develop the capabilities of its Department of Collective Bargaining Services, providing additional funds for that purpose, and continue its support for the disputes settlement plan and productivity/quality of work life project of IMI's Labor/Management Relations program.

Membership Services

It should become IU policy to provide all members with services that they need and which can be offered on a cost-efficient basis.

BAC should establish an International Health and Welfare Fund, programs to further member mobility through the portability of benefits, a computerized job referral service, broader opportunities for group purchasing of goods and services by our members, and more participation by local unions in the International Pension Fund. The IU should expand its member communications program technologically, to include the latest and most effective communications media, and financially, by providing for this purpose $1.2 million annually. It should also establish a $700,000-per-year member education program built around "study circles" for members and their families and leadership courses for local officers.

Organizing and Membership

It must be the policy of the IU to organize into membership all craftsmen and workers in the trowel trades and related industry activities such as manufacturing of masonry products so that pools of non-union masonry workers will be eliminated, all trowel trades craftsmen and allied workers will enjoy the privileges and benefits of BAC membership, and the masonry industry will enjoy the advantages of unity and progress. To achieve the fulfillment of this policy, the IU should:

- As a first phase in a new organizing effort, launch a five-year, $7.5 million organizing program funded in its first three years by a special $10 per member per year assessment.

- Merge into BAC all other trowel trades unions and related groups of workers.
- Assume jurisdiction for related work beyond traditional masonry boundaries, including new wall systems and components, products and methods.

The committee believes that the IU's new organizing effort must place great emphasis on the residential market, take advantage of the newest technology and concepts, be thoroughly coordinated with all other IU programs and activities, and recognize the importance of foremen who understand the value of BAC membership and support the principles of collective bargaining.

Structure, Administration and Management of BAC

The IU must adopt and implement structural changes that will enable our Union and its resources to be administered and managed more effectively, respond to differing regional needs and opportunities, and deliver services more efficiently to all members, regardless of their location or the size and nature of their local union. These changes must include:

- Establishment of a regional structure and management system for the Union and related joint programs in coordination with employer groups.
- Regionalization of the IU Executive Council by including regionally-elected business agents as regional vice presidents, craft- or division-elected business agents as craft or division vice presidents, and regional director positions filled by current regional vice presidents.
- Establishment of a financial management and accounting unit for all BAC and related collectively-bargained and industry programs, and creation of working capital and sinking funds to anticipate programs' needs and fund short-term operating deficits.
- Creation and funding at a cost of $200,000 per year of IU leadership development programs.
- Motivation of local unions to move quickly to establish IU dues check-offs in order to help resolve BAC's intermediate cash flow problem.
- Establishment where needed of state/provincial administrative units to relieve local unions of administrative tasks and assure the effective delivery of services to all members.

Table 3–1
Summary of BAC's Cost of Recommendations

Program	Source of Funds	Annual Amount
Advertising and promotion	Collective bargaining	$20 million
Research and development	Collective bargaining	20 million
Training	Collective bargaining	20 million
Communications	Dues	1.2 million
External communications	Dues	250,000
Education program	Dues	700,000
Organizing	Special assessment	1.5 million
Political action	Voluntary contributions	1.6 million
Political/legislative	Dues	150,000
Collective bargaining	Dues	150,000
Leadership development	Dues	200,000
Total		$65.75 million

- Development of a system to evaluate the performance of local unions and officers and help them to establish goals and objectives and improve their operations.

The Project 2000 Committee concluded after many meetings, much discussion and a great deal of hard work that while not all of these recommendations can be implemented at once, all of them must be implemented in the near term future in order to assure the future of the Union. The implementation of these recommendations ultimately will depend on the support of our members, and we urge all of our officers and leaders to begin immediately to discuss these proposals with our members and provide opportunities for our members to participate in the shaping and execution of these plans. Obviously we will have to significantly adjust our method of operation to achieve the objectives set by the Committee. Finally, we commend to all BAC members and officers who read this report the conviction that our Union must earn its right to exist, that the primary means of earning this right is through service, and that the best way to demonstrate our accomplishment will be to strive for a standard of excellence in all that we say and do. [See table 3–1.]

Notes

1. For reference to the development of the Bricklayers, see Lloyd Ulman, *The Rise of the National Trade Union: The Development and Significance of the Struc-*

ture, Governing Institutions, and Economic Policies (Cambridge: Harvard University Press, 1955). Also see Harry C. Bates, *Bricklayers' Century of Craftsmanship: A History of the Bricklayers, Masons and Plasterers' International Union of America* (Washington, D.C.: Bricklayers, Masons and Plasterers' International Union of America, 1955).

2. *Project 2000 Committee, Report and Recommendations, International Union of Bricklayers and Allied Craftsmen* (Washington, D.C., International Union of Bricklayers and Allied Craftsmen, 1985).

3. I testified before the committee.

4. *Project 2000 Committee, Report*, pp. 102–105.

CASE 3
PARTIAL PLANNING STEPS: A VARIETY
OF ILLUSTRATIONS

Short of comprehensive strategic planning of the sort illustrated by the CWA and the BAC, a labor organization may develop a plan for a subordinate body or may concentrate on one of the elements of planning, such as environmental analysis, the reshaping of its structure, or a plan to select or train officers at various levels in the union. Some of these instances will be identified, and several other issues are briefly discussed.

The Massachusetts/AFL-CIO held a conference[1] with affiliated local unions and with the assistance of national labor leaders and academics to spread the reports of the AFL-CIO Committee on the Evolution of Work, *The Future of Work* (August 1983) and *The Changing Situation of Workers and Their Unions* (February 1985). A series of regional meetings with central labor councils was planned to extend the ideas to local unions and members.

Labor organizations over the years have on occasion prepared, or have had outside experts prepare, reports with recommendations on major changes in the environment confronting the union in collective bargaining or on new issues or proposals that may be raised in negotiations or on some unresolved policy issue. The United Steelworkers of America, confronted with extraordinary problems of declining employment and membership, international competition, and demands from basic steel companies for further concessions, commissioned a major study as part of its preparation for the 1986 negotiations.[2]

A number of international unions and the AFL-CIO have issued reports or manuals to meet urgent problems and provide guidance to local unions and members. The United Food and Commercial Workers, confronted with widespread plant and store shutdowns, issued an Economic Dislocation Manual.[3] The CWA also developed a detailed program to assist unemployed members.[4] In a different area, an AFL-CIO report seeks to encourage investments of union pension funds more in accord with the needs and interests of union members. The report was prepared after substantial study and consultation with a wide range of experts in the United States and abroad.[5] A manual on internal organizing provides detailed procedures and suggestions.[6]

Notes

1. *Massachusetts Unions and the Future of Work: A Report on the Conference Presented by the Massachusetts AFL/CIO* (February 1986).
2. *Confronting the Crisis: The Challenge for Labor: Report to United Steelworkers of America, AFL-CIO-CLC, December 16, 1985* (New York: Locker/ Abrecht Associates, 1985).
3. United Food and Commercial Workers International Union, *UFCW Economic Dislocation Manual*, (Washington, D.C., 1985).
4. Communication Workers of America, *Assisting Displaced Workers: A Local Union Program for Unemployed Members* (Washington, D.C.: CWA, 1985).
5. AFL-CIO *Investment of Union Pension Funds* (Washington, D.C.: AFL-CIO, 1981).
6. AFL-CIO, *Numbers That Count: A Manual on Internal Organizing* (Washington, D.C.: AFL-CIO, June 1988).

CASE 4
PROGRAM TO RESTRUCTURE THE
INTERNATIONAL UNION

At its eighteenth general convention in 1984, President John J. Sweeney introduced a program to restructure the Service Employees International Union (SEIU).[1] The plan contained the following elements:

1. Establish six industry divisions: building service, health care, public sector, clerical, professional and industrial, and allied choices.
2. Establish regional offices in the United States and Canada.
3. Establish a Canadian desk at the international headquarters with the responsibility to see that all programs are tailored for the Canadian membership.
4. Computerize local union offices and tie them to the computer facilities of the international union.

The program also provided for a greatly expanded international union organizing effort, with a concentration on recruiting minorities, blacks, Hispanics, and women in these organizing posts. In addition to restructuring and organizing, President Sweeney outlined additional areas of improvement: expansion of training and education programs for the international staff, communications on an industry basis with the development of specialized newsletters and membership publications for the divisions, expansion of the safety and health program, expansion of activities in the area of pay equity, increase in political efforts, expansion in the legislative department to handle better the variety of legislative interests that the union must address, expansion of efforts in the area of health care cost containment, and increased education and training of local union pension fund trustees to better deal with the complex problems of pension funds.

In order to fund these expanded programs, the delegates approved a significant per capita increase from $2.55 per month to an additional $1.25 per month over the following four years.

Note

1. See Bureau of National Affairs, *Daily Labor Report,* May 16, 1984, pp. A-2, A-3, AFL-CIO, CLC, *Proceedings of the Eighteenth Convention of the Service Employees International Union,* May 13–17, 1984, pp. xv, 194–211.

CASE 5

GENERAL MOTORS AND UAW:
PLANNING FOR JOB SECURITY
AND OPERATIONAL EFFECTIVENESS

In some situations the parties to collective bargaining agreements may have specific common objectives, and a joint strategic plan may be essential to achieve the common purpose.[1]

The 1987 national agreement between General Motors and the United Autoworkers of America (UAW) included the following memorandum:

> The Corporation and the Union recognize that quality and operating efficiency are inextricably wed to job security, and that a high level of quality and operating efficiency requires mutual respect and recognition of each other's problems and concerns. Accordingly, an addition to the Local JOBS committee's responsibilities for the JOBS Program and participation in discussions in related Letters of Understanding, each committee will focus on cooperative efforts toward our common goal to improve the effectiveness of operations and remove barriers to improvements, increase job opportunities and fully utilize the workforce. The local com-

mittees will jointly develop a plan through an exhaustive analysis of the location's operational efficiency.

The manual that was jointly developed describes a process for joint local committees to plan toward the objective of improved effectiveness of operations and job security and specifies steps to achieve these goals.

Note

1. *Planning for Success, Job Security and Operational Effectiveness: General Motors and UAW, 1988.* The joint pamphlet was developed for local jobs committees. (Detroit, Michigan: General Motors and UAW, 1988).

CASE 6
LABOR ORGANIZATION MERGERS AND STRATEGIC DECISIONS

In the world of business, the merger of companies or the purchase or sale of component parts or even total enterprises is a major focus of strategic planning. It is a major means of exercising the executive function of shaping or reshaping the structure of an organization.[1]

Since the late 1970s there has been an acceleration in the extent of mergers among national labor organizations beyond the rate that took place in the quarter-century after the AFL-CIO merger, more out of necessity and the economics of union operations than from the ideology of solidarity (table 3–2).[2] The costs of providing services to members and the range of professional, legal, and representational services that members may desire has grown to such an extent that costs are in excess of dues capacity in many smaller unions or those with declining membership. Still, many smaller units of crafts, industrial sectors, or occupations prefer the unity and coherence that comes from having their own organization. Often mergers involve means to preserve such independence while securing the advantages of larger scale. It is unclear what configurations of labor organizations in occupations, crafts, and industries are optimal for union growth and service to members.

This labor merger movement has also been taking place among local unions. Consolidation is also reflected in the formation or strengthening of district councils, joint boards, regional offices, departments, internal divisions (as in the case of the SEIU), or other intermediate bodies of union governance or coordination. The extent of local union mergers is reflected in the experience of the Carpenters, which had about 3,000 local unions in the 1960s and

Table 3–2

Chronology of Labor Organization Mergers, January 1979–April 1984

Date	Organization and Affiliation[a]	Membership at Time of Merger
1979		
January	International Typographical Union (AFL–CIO)	81,300
	International Mailers Union (Ind.)	3,100
March	Amalgamated Clothing and Textile Workers Union (AFL–CIO)	475,000
	United Shoe Workers of America (AFL–CIO)	25,000
June	Retail Clerks International Union (AFL–CIO)	735,000
	Amalgamated Meat Cutters and Butcher Workmen of North America (AFL–CIO)	500,000
	Formed the United Food and Commercial Workers International Union (AFL–CIO)	
	International Union, United Automobile, Aerospace and Agricultural Implement Workers of America (AFL–CIO)	1,499,000
	Distributive Workers of America (Ind.)	35,000
August	International Brotherhood of Carpenters and Joiners of America (AFL–CIO)	750,000
	The Wood, Wire and Metal Lathers International Union (AFL–CIO)	11,000
1980		
January	Tile, Marble and Terrazzo Finishers and Shopmen International Union (AFL–CIO)	7,000
	The Granite Cutters International Association of America (AFL–CIO)	2,300
June	Brotherhood of Railway, Airline and Steamship Clerks, Freight Handlers, Express and Station Employees (AFL–CIO)	170,000
	The American Railway and Airway Supervisors Association (AFL–CIO)	8,000
July	Service Employees International Union (AFL–CIO)	625,500
	International Jewelry Workers' Union (AFL–CIO)	10,000
September	United Food and Commercial Workers International Union (AFL–CIO)	1,300,000
	Barbers, Beauticians and Allied Industries International Association (AFL–CIO)	27,000
October	International Longshoremen's and Warehousemen's Union (Ind.)	64,000
	Inland Boatmen's Union of the Pacific (Ind.)	4,000
November	Service Employees International Union (AFL–CIO)	635,500
	Oregon State Employees Association (AGE)[b]	14,500
1981		
January	International Organization of Masters, Mates and Pilots (Marine Division—ILA[3] (AFL–CIO)	9,000
	American Radio Association (AFL–CIO)	473
September	Aluminum Workers International Union (AFL–CIO)	27,000
	The United Brick and Clay Workers of America (AFL–CIO)	15,000
	Formed the Aluminum, Brick and Clay Workers International Union (AFL–CIO)	
November	United Food and Commercial Workers International Union (AFL–CIO)	1,300,000
	United Retail Workers Union (Ind.)	22,000
1982		
July	Glass Bottle Blowers of the United States and Canada (AFL–CIO)	80,000
	International Brotherhood of Pottery and Allied Workers (AFL–CIO)	11,000
September	Aluminum, Brick and Clay Workers International Union (AFL–CIO)	40,000
	United Glass and Ceramic Workers of North America (AFL–CIO)	28,000
	Formed the Aluminum, Brick and Glass Workers International Union (AFL–CIO)	

Table 3–2 continued

Date	Organization and Affiliation[a]	Membership at Time of Merger
1982		
October	American Federation of State, County and Municipal Employees (AFL–CIO)	1,100,000
	Arizona Public Employees Association (AGE)	7,500
November	Hotel Employees and Restaurant Employees International Union (AFL–CIO)	400,000
	International Production, Service and Sales Union (Ind.)	18,000
December	Service Employees International Union (AFL–CIO)	650,000
	National Association of Government Employees (Ind.)	100,000
	Amalgamated Clothing and Textile Workers Union (AFL–CIO)	410,000
	United Hatters, Cap and Millinery Workers International Union (AFL–CIO)	8,000
1983		
May	American Federation of State, County and Municipal Employees (AFL–CIO)	1,130,000
	Ohio Civil Service Employees Association, Inc. (AGE)	17,000
July	International Printing and Graphic Communications Union (AFL–CIO)	112,000
	Graphic Arts International Union (AFL–CIO)	82,500
	Formed the Graphic Communications International Union	
August	Brotherhood of Railway, Airline and Steamship Clerks, Freight Handlers, Express and Station Employees (AFL–CIO)	178,000
	Western Railway Supervisors Association (Ind.)	325
October	United Food and Commercial Workers International Union (AFL–CIO)	1,300,000
	Insurance Workers International Union (AFL–CIO)	15,000
December	American Federation of Government Employees (AFL–CIO)	255,000
	National Association of Government Inspectors and Quality Assurance Personnel (Ind.)	800
1984		
February	Service Employees International Union (AFL–CIO)	750,000
	California State Employees Association (AGE)	50,000
	American Federation of State, County and Municipal Employees (AFL–CIO)	1,130,000
	Ohio Association of Public School Employees (Ind.)	25,000
March	International Union, United Automobile, Aerospace and Agricultural Implement Workers of America (AFL–CIO)	1,100,000
	Brewery Workers Local 9 (A directly affiliated local of the AFL–CIO)	2,400
April	International Brotherhood of Boilermakers, Iron Ship Builders, Blacksmiths, Forgers and Helpers (AFL–CIO)	134,000
	United Cement, Lime and Gypsum Workers International Union (AFL–CIO)	29,000
	Communications Workers of America (AFL–CIO)	550,500
	West Virginia Public Employees Association (Ind.)	1,500

Source: Larry T. Adams, "Labor Organization Mergers, 1979–84: Adapting to Change," *Monthly Labor Review,* (September 1984), pp. 23–24.

Note: This table reflects all mergers known to the Bureau of Labor Statistics as of June 30, 1984.

[a]Affiliations are designated as AFL–CIO; Ind. (independent); and AGE (Assembly of Government Employees).

[b]These organizations disaffiliated with the AGE just prior to, or at the time of, merging.

[c]International Longshoremen's Association.

currently reports approximately 1,700, although some of the reduction no doubt reflects the disappearance of some smaller locals and other factors.

The following excerpts from an article in the *Monthly Labor Review* describe the acceleration on national union mergers in the 1980s.[3]

Although the constitution of the AFL-CIO strongly endorses the "elimination of conflicting and duplicating organizations and jurisdictions through the process of . . . voluntary mergers," only 20 mergers took place between 1955 and 1965. Disappointed at the slow rate of amalgamation, George Meany declared in December 1965, "I . . . strongly suggest that the responsible officers of many unions, who by all logic and commonsense should merge, might well take a broader look at the union as an instrument of progress for working people rather than an institution devoted to its own perpetuation for the sake of sentiment and tradition."[4] The pace of mergers remained slow for the next 2 years, but became brisk between 1968 and 1972, with 19 mergers occurring. Six years of modest merger activity followed. However, the pace picked up again in 1979 and continued through the date of this study.

Although unity has always been a philosophical goal of organized labor, practical considerations usually provide the impetus for merger. Some labor organizations merge because of costly jurisdictional disputes or the need to gain a strong and unified voice in collective bargaining. Others choose merger because they cannot survive in the face of dwindling membership and dues income stemming with employment loss resulting from import competition, recession, technological change, or employer relocation.

A few mergers involve relatively equal organizations joining to form a new entity, but most are the result of an absorption of a small labor organization by a much larger one. But regardless of the type of merger, an agreement of affiliation must be reached regarding organizational structure, election and terms of office, bylaws, and union dues that will accommodate the individual functions and philosophies of the organizations. An acceptable means of sharing authority and control by officers of both organizations must be determined. For organizations with strong craft traditions, the issues of craft identity and jurisdiction must be dealt with. When these and other issues are not resolved, potential mergers fail. Merger is a difficult process requiring delicate negotiations, patience, and sensitivity to personal and institutional sensibilities. Although mergers may be good for the labor movement in general, they usually occur when the economic and institutional problems that create the need to merge outweigh the problems of satisfying that need.

Mergers involving employee associations occur, in part, for reasons similar to those influencing mergers by traditional labor unions, but there are significant historical and legal differences. Between 1960 and mid-

1984, when State and local government employment more than doubled, many States passed laws granting public employees the right to organize and bargain collectively. Expanding their functions beyond the traditional lobbying and merit system activities, many national professional groups and State employee associations began to organize workers, petition for representation elections, and engage in collective bargaining.[5] The blessings of these changes were mixed. Even where the legal right to organize and negotiate collective bargaining agreements had been conferred, many State labor laws did not provide for or proscribed requirements that workers represented by an association for bargaining join and pay dues or a service charge. As a result, many associations were required to represent all workers in a bargaining unit while operating on a limited budget. Other associations, covered by stronger security provisions, were able to secure adequate financial resources only to be confronted with costly jurisdictional challenges from stronger national labor organizations. For many of these public employee associations, merger with a national labor organization is the most effective way to increase their strength and ensure their future.

Mergers of labor organizations (both unions and employee associations) are, in general, precipitated and molded by a broad set of economic, institutional, legal, and social factors. The blend of these issues is unique to each merger situation, and the resulting amalgamation is also unique. . . .

Merger is perhaps the most efficient method for a labor organization to increase membership and financial resources. Many organizations that have traditionally represented workers in industries and occupations now adversely affected by recession, imports, plant relocation, technological change, and other disruptions are actively seeking to absorb small related organizations. They also seek to expand their jurisdictions to the growing or stable areas of the economy such as service industries and the public sector. However, these unions may experience conflict with organizations that already represent workers in these areas and are eager to maintain and expand their own jurisdictions. With many large labor organizations representing both public and private sector workers actively courting a limited number of merger partners, rivalries have developed. . . .

The process of labor organizations striving to adapt, survive, and prosper within the changing configuration of the U.S. economy is likely to keep merger activity fast-paced and highly competitive.

Notes

1. For historical perspective, see Alfred D. Chandler, Jr., *The Visible Hand: The Managerial Revolution in American Business* (Cambridge: Belknap Press of Harvard

University Press, 1972), pp. 315–344, 484–500; John R. Meyer and James M. Gustafson, eds., *The U.S. Business Corporation: An Institution in Transition* (Cambridge, Mass.: Ballinger, 1988).

2. See Gideon Chitayat, *Trade Union Mergers and Labor Conglomerates* (New York: Praeger, 1979).

3. Larry T. Adams, "Labor Organization Mergers 1979–84: Adapting to Change," *Monthly Labor Review* (September 1984): 21–27.

4. *Proceedings of the Sixth Constitutional Convention of the AFL-CIO*, December 9, 1965, p. 21.

5. The American Nurses Association and the Arizona Public Employees Association are examples of national professional and state employee associations.

Questions

1. Under what circumstances is it appropriate for a labor organization to seek to develop a comprehensive strategic plan? How often should such a plan be reviewed and altered? Is such a strategic plan a continuing feature of union governance?

2. In the CWA case the president chaired the committee, while in the case of the Bricklayers, local business agents served on the committee and international union officers were not members. What factors affect the composition of such a committee?

3. Can a strategic plan for a labor organization be developed effectively without the involvement or participation of employers involved in collective bargaining? To what extent do changes in the union involve changes in policy among employers? In what areas is it appropriate to involve employers?

4. Strategic planning on a comprehensive scale appears to involve considerations of union finances. Why are such considerations significant? Are they determinative?

5. What procedures are necessary and appropriate to involve local unions and members in the strategic planning process since their support is likely to be essential to make major changes, including financial changes, in the organization?

6. Develop and draft a strategic plan for a labor organization starting with an environmental assessment relevant to the particular union.

7. What are the principal features of an environmental analysis, an essential component of strategic planning? Contrast the union of the future environment depicted by the CWA and by the BCA. How do you account for these differences? Are they compatible?

8. Any serious consideration of a merger involves negotiations that appear to contain elements of strategic planning. Some mergers are an option; others reflect the only alternative for an organization. What determines synergism among labor organizations?

9. To what extent is merger among labor organizations primarily a matter of political contest for leadership posts? To what extent are salary scales of staff, pension plans, dues levels and per capita payments, and so on serious considerations?

10. Discuss and illustrate how history, traditions, and ideology of a labor organization influence current major decisions (such as involved in strategic planning and merger) as compared to the role of economic and financial considerations.

11. Identify some of the problems that arise in an international union in strategic planning by virtue of membership in both Canada and the United States.

Part II
The Institutional Setting
of Decisions

4

The Federation and the Constituent National Unions

From its formation in the 1880s the AFL adopted two fundamental constitutional principles governing the relationship between the constituent national unions and the federation. (The term *national union* is used to denote either a national or an international union. National unions with affiliates in the United States that also have affiliates in Canada or, in a few cases, Latin America or territories outside the United States often designate themselves as international unions.) These principles have shaped the Federation to this day in significant ways, including defining the basic constitutional conflict between the AFL and the CIO in the period 1935–1955. The evolution of these principles reflects a changing federation and a larger role of government in union affairs.

1880–1935

The first constitutional principle was the autonomy of each constituent national union. From the outset the constitution stated that an object of the Federation was "the establishment of National and International Trade Unions, based upon a strict recognition of the autonomy of each trade, and the promotion and advancement of such bodies." The Federation was not to intervene or involve itself in the internal affairs of a national union, its elections of officers, its collective bargaining, or its supervision of local unions and members. Autonomy did not preclude, or course, a constituent national union seeking support of the Federation in a strike or boycott against employers, in community affairs, or to secure favorable legislation or administrative action. Indeed such assistance was a reflection of solidarity and a major purpose of the Federation. The principle of autonomy, however, was at the center of conflicts within the Federation over allegations that some affiliates were dominated by a criminal element or by the Communist party or other political ideology. Were there limits to autonomy, and if so, where should they be drawn and by whom?

The second constitutional principle was exclusive jurisdiction: each affiliated national union should have a prescribed job territory within which to operate. Each affiliate should refrain from invading or trespassing the exclusive jurisdiction of another affiliate. Jurisdiction was clearly analogous to a property right with a constitutional guarantee against encroachment. The constitutional language was as follows:

> No charter shall be granted by the American Federation of Labor to any National, International, Trade or Federal Labor Union without a positive and clear definition of the trade jurisdiction claimed by the applicant, and the charter shall not be granted if the jurisdiction claimed is a trespass on the jurisdiction of existing affiliated unions, without the written consent of such unions; no affiliated International, National, or Local Union shall be permitted to change its title or name, if any trespass is made thereby on the jurisdiction of an affiliated organization, without having first obtained the consent and approval of a convention of the American Federation of Labor; and it is further provided, that should any of the members of such National, International, Trade or Federal Labor Union work at any other vocation, trade or profession, they shall join the union of such vocation, trade, or profession, provided such are organized and affiliated with the American Federation of Labor.

Workers were expected to join the union that the Federation had designated as having exclusive jurisdiction over the job territory in which the worker was employed and even to shift to that union if already a member of a different union. The principle was not that a worker join the union of his or her choice or the union that a majority of workers, in some unit determined by a government agency, voted for in an election. Thus the principle of exclusive jurisdiction was at once a constitutional contract between the constituent national unions and the Federation incorporated in a charter and at the same time a direction to individual workers as to the labor organizations they should join, if affiliated with the AFL.

The AFL regarded the organization of a dual or rival union—whether that affiliate had the workers organized under a collective agreement or not—as a serious violation of the principle of exclusive jurisdiction. Indeed the CIO unions were charged with dual unionism, tried, suspended, and expelled from the AFL in 1936–1938.

John P. Frey, president of the AFL Metal Trades Department filed this charge on July 15, 1936:

1. The Committee for Industrial Organization is a dual organization functioning within the American Federation of Labor as such and in its administrative activities it is clearly competing as a rival organization with the American Federation of Labor.

    The final authority in the American Federation of Labor on questions of jurisdiction is the Executive Council and the conventions of the

American Federation of Labor. The Committee for Industrial Organization has set itself up as a dual authority, and is now engaged in an effort to determine questions of jurisdiction and to make decisions which are in direct conflict with those of the Executive Council of the American Federation of Labor. . . .

3. Each of the organizations herein named which holds membership in the Committee for Industrial Organization has violated the contract which each of them entered into with the American Federation of Labor when it was granted certificates of affiliation.[1]

The principle of exclusive jurisdiction was administered solely by the AFL through its annual conventions and the executive council. The government, outside neutrals, and arbitrators had no role. The only sanctions the Federation had to enforce its decisions were the moral force of the organization or expulsion from the AFL for noncompliance. These measures were not effective in some disputes over jurisdiction, particularly with large affiliates, and many disputes continued for years. On some occasions major affiliates withdrew to protest a decision, ceasing per capita payments to the Federation.

1935–1955

The Wagner Act in 1935 placed in the National Labor Relations Board (NLRB) the authority to decide the appropriate bargaining unit, such as between a plantwide unit or a number of separate craft units. It excluded certain supervisory employees from any units, and it provided employers and the courts with a role in unit determination. Sections 9(a) and (b) of the act provided:

(a) Representatives designated or selected for the purposes of collective bargaining by the majority of the employees in a unit appropriate for such purposes, shall be the exclusive representatives of all the employees in such unit for the purposes of collective bargaining in respect to rates of pay, wages, hours of employment, or other conditions of employment. . . .

(b) The Board shall decide in each case whether, in order to assure to employees the fullest freedom in exercising the rights guaranteed by this Act, the most appropriate for the purposes of collective bargaining shall be the employer unit, craft unit, plant unit, or subdivision thereof.

In the great debate on industrial unionism at the 1935 AFL convention, Matthew Woll recognized the significance of the new legislation, particularly in a divided labor movement: "Bear in mind that we now have legislation on our books which does not make us the sole factor in determining the form and character of organization that shall hereafter prevail in the labor movement. That power, to a large degree, has now been lodged in a Federal Government agency."

Beyond the question of what labor organization a worker shall join or what the job or occupational contour of a bargaining unit shall be, the Taft-Haftley Act (1947) extended the role of the NLRB to deal with the question of the occupation or craft that is entitled to perform specified work operations. In section 10(k) the board was authorized to determine work jurisdiction disputes in further erosion of the exclusive jurisdiction principle of the Federation:

> Whenever it is charged that any person has engaged in an unfair labor practice within the meaning of paragraph (4)(D) of Section 8(b), the Board is empowered and directed to hear and determine the dispute out of which such unfair labor practice shall have arisen, unless, within ten days after notice that such charge has been filed, the parties to such dispute submit to the Board satisfactory evidence that they have adjusted, or agreed upon methods for the voluntary adjustment of the dispute.

Between 1935 and 1955 the AFL continued with its historical constitutional principle of exclusive jurisdiction. There had always been deviations, particularly in some industries, between charter jurisdiction and actual representation of workers and their job territory. These differences were exacerbated by the intense conflict for representation rights between AFL and CIO unions and by unit determinations of the NLRB. The private principle of exclusive jurisdiction in actual practice, outside of a few sectors such as construction and railroads, yielded to governmental administration of bargaining unit determinations.

The CIO introduced the Internal Disputes Plan, which provided for an outside umpire (arbitrator) to determine which of competing CIO unions in a prospective NLRB representation election would most effectively represent the workers and required that other CIO union contestants, in compliance with the award, withdraw from the election, leaving one CIO union to confront AFL, independent union, or nonunion choices on the ballot.

The AFL's Building and Construction Trades Department and national contractor associations jointly established a private machinery in 1948 with an outside umpire to resolve work assignment disputes in that industry. The National Joint Board for the Settlement of Jurisdictional Disputes, reorganized as the Impartial Jurisdictional Disputes Board in 1973, was empowered to resolve disputes on particular projects and to mediate and to mandate a national decision on a contested issue. Since the NLRB has held representation elections relatively infrequently in construction and in view of the limited duration of work on construction sites and the specialized work operations of many contractors, the traditional concepts of exclusive jurisdiction have retained much of their imprint in this industry. Traditional jurisdictional concepts remain an active factor in the processes by which contractors make work assignments and union officials and members respond. Conflicts in decisions between the private machinery and the NLRB were not a serious problem until after the 1960s.

1955–1980s

The constitution of the merged federation, AFL-CIO, sought to provide an internal means to resolve conflicts between the national unions affiliated previously with both federations, as well as to eliminate the inconsistency between the traditional doctrine of exclusive representation of the AFL, in effect destroyed by the Wagner Act (1935) and the Taft-Hartley Act (1947), and the public policy of choice by workers among unions determined by elections conducted by government.

The AFL-CIO constitution substituted the concept of established bargaining representative for the historical concept of exclusive jurisdiction. It stated: "Each affiliate shall respect the established collective bargaining relationship of every other affiliate. No affiliate shall organize or attempt to represent employees as to whom an established collective bargaining relationship exists with any other affiliate." The constitution also provided, in Article XX, for an outside umpire (arbitrator) to make determinations as to whether an affiliate violated this provision by various forms of raiding an established collective bargaining relationship. An outside mediation step before the umpire has also been introduced. The determination of the umpire is subject to review and may be overturned by the executive council of the AFL-CIO. Any affiliate found by the council to be in noncompliance may be subject to withdrawal of the protection of the no-raiding provisions of the constitution and other sanctions.

In practice the national unions in the Federation have respected the established collective bargaining relationship of other affiliates during the duration of a collective agreement in conforming with public law and even when the agreement is open, at which time public law permits a challenge or a raid. The established collective bargaining relationships of labor organizations outside the Federation need not be respected by AFL-CIO affiliates.

The AFL-CIO constitution in 1955 also introduced the concept of organizing jurisdiction and stated that each affiliate retain the same organizing jurisdiction that it had before the merger. This principle did little to restrain competition among federation affiliates for new bargaining units since there was no operative definition of organizing jurisdictions or procedures to implement the principle. In 1986, however, the AFL-CIO established a procedure for determining organizing responsibilities, except for construction, with umpires (initially retired national union presidents) to determine which affiliate shall have the sole right to seek to become the exclusive representative of the employee group in question for a period of one year. Article XXI of the AFL-CIO constitution now provides for organizing responsibility procedures. Such procedures had been recommended in a February 1985 AFL-CIO report.

The standards to be applied by the Umpire are as follows. If the Umpire finds either:

1. that one affiliate which is a party to the case began a full-fledged organizing drive adequate to organize the employee group significantly before any other affiliate and that affiliate has a reasonable chance of successfully organizing the employee group; or if this standard does not apply,

2. that one affiliate is significantly more likely to obtain majority support from the employee group than any other affiliate which received formal notice of the case or which intervened and participated as a party, then, the Umpire shall enter an award so stating.[2]

The procedure also specifies relevant factors the umpire shall consider in assessing an affiliate's likelihood of success in organizing an employee group, such as the extent of current support; support from other affiliates in a co-ordinated organizing campaign; experience with the same employer; resources already expended, budgeted, or projected to be expended on the organizing; and existing membership and bargaining relationship with the same employer.

In 1951 the CIO had adopted an agreement governing organizational disputes that would decide which of its affiliates should be on a representation ballot to increase the opportunity for one of them to win an election against AFL unions or no-votes. The plan was continued under the Industrial Union Department of the merged federation.

There have thus been three periods over the past century in the general evolution of the constitutional relationship between the Federation and its affiliate unions and in the principles that affect the affiliation of workers to particular unions.

From the 1880s to 1935 was the era of exclusive jurisdiction in which each affiliate had by charter a positive and clear definition of trade jurisdiction, and workers were expected to join the union with the assigned job territory or jurisdiction. These principles were administered solely by the Federation, and only private means of enforcement were available.

The years 1935–1955 were a period in which the NLRB came to determine bargaining units or election districts and after 1947 to determine work jurisdiction disputes. These actions were at times totally inconsistent with the exclusion jurisdiction concepts of the Federation. These differences were exacerbated by the conflicts and competition for collective agreements and members between the AFL and CIO unions and among unions in the Federation. The legal force of administrative agencies and the courts largely replaced the voluntarism of the labor movement in settling internal disputes over exclusive jurisdiction.

With the 1955 merger of the AFL and the CIO, the concept of established bargaining relationship replaced exclusive jurisdiction as the basic principle governing the relationships among affiliates. The principle helped to establish effective private internal processes in the Federation and to eliminate conflict between internal processes and public policy processes. Since 1986 the Federation has also sought not only to constrain competition among affiliates over established collective bargaining relationships but also over the organizing of unorganized units or those outside the Federation.

Notes

1. American Federation of Labor, *AF of L vs. C.I.O., The Record*, (Washington, D.C., A.F.L., November 20, 1939, pp. 18–19).
2. Statement by the AFL-CIO Executive Council, *Procedure for Determining Organizing Responsibilities*, February 18, 1986, pp. 2–3.

Suggested Reading

A.F. of L. vs. C.I.O., The Record (Washington, D.C.: American Federation of Labor, November 20, 1939).
The Changing Situation of Workers and Their Unions, Report by the AFL-CIO Committee on the Evolution of Work (Washington, D.C.: AFL-CIO, February 1985).
John T. Dunlop, "Structural Changes in the American Labor Movement and Industrial Relations System," *Proceedings of the Ninth Annual Meeting, Industrial Relations Research Association*, December 28–29, 1956, pp. 12–32.
John T. Dunlop, *Dispute Resolution, Negotiation and Consensus Building* (Dover, Mass.: Auburn House, 1984), pp. 194–204.
Walter Galenson, *The CIO Challenge to the AFL: A History of the American Labor Movement, 1935–1941* (Cambridge: Harvard University Press, 1960), pp. 3–74.
Walter Galenson, *The United Brotherhood of Carpenters: The First Hundred Years* (Cambridge: Harvard University Press, 1983).
Arthur J. Goldberg, *AFL-CIO Labor United* (New York: McGraw-Hill, 1956), pp. 103–118, 141–154.
Mark Perlman, *The Machinists: A Study in American Trade Unionism* (Cambridge: Harvard University Press, 1961).

CASE 1
THE LIMITS OF AUTONOMY

At the 1940 Convention of the AFL, the newly returned International Ladies Garment Workers' Union, headed by David Dubinsky, introduced a resolution:

> Resolved (1) That the American Federation of Labor, through its Executive Council, or any agency authorized by it have summary power to order the removal by any national or international union affiliated with it, of any officer or officers convicted of any offense involving moral turpitude or conviction of bringing their official positions in their unions for personal gain, in all cases where such national or international unions or federal locals have failed to do so. . . .
>
> (3) That whenever any union fails to institute proceedings in accordance with its constitution against any officers charged with the above acts, the AFL shall use its full moral force to compel the filing of charges and the holding of a hearing upon the same.

The executive council and the convention expressed full accord with the purpose "to maintain a high moral standard in our trade union movement, and that we definitely disavow racketeering and gangsterism, and that we want none of it in our movement." Further: "Your Committee, without qualification, condemns the action of trade union officials who use their position of trust, confidence and high responsibility, for the purpose of exploiting those whom they represent, the employers and the public, for their private gain."

But the executive council and the convention rejected the proposed resolution in language that contained the following statements:

> We must keep in mind that the American Federation of Labor is a federation of self-governing national, and international unions who have been guaranteed their right to self-government, which includes their election and selection of officers and control over their conduct.
>
> Our national and international unions are autonomous bodies, chartered by the American Federation of Labor, governed by their own laws and administered by the officers of said organizations. We respect the rights of the membership of these unions to administer their own affairs.

The 1955 constitution of the merged Federation in Article VIII, section 7, includes the following provision:

> It is a basic principle of this Federation that it must be and remain free from any and all corrupt influences and from the undermining efforts of communist, fascist or other totalitarian agencies who are opposed to the

basic principles of our democracy and of free and democratic trade unions. The Executive Council, when requested to do so by the President or by any other member of the Executive Council, shall have the power to conduct an investigation, directly or through an appropriate standing or special committee appointed by the President. . . . Upon completion of such an investigation, including hearings if requested, the Executive Council shall have authority to make recommendations or give directions to the affiliate involved and shall have the further authority upon a two-thirds vote, to suspend any affiliate found guilty of a violation of this section.

Questions

1. What does it mean to state that the national unions are autonomous affiliates of the Federation? Are there any limits to autonomy? Has autonomy been applied to large and small unions?

2. The Teamsters' union was expelled from the Federation in 1957 and returned in 1988. Did expulsion adversely affect the Teamsters' union? Did separation from the Teamsters help or adversely affect the Federation?

3. The internal procedures of the merged Federation to deal with charges of corruption or communist domination have not been used since 1957. Why not? The Federation appears to rely, as to corruption, on the public processes of the Landrum-Griffin statute (1957) or other public laws. Is this an adequate standard?

4. At what stage from discovery to conviction and denial of all appeals in the courts should a union official be removed from office? What considerations enter into this judgment?

Note

1. *The Changing Situation of Workers and Their Unions*, Report by the AFL-CIO Committee on the Evolution of Work (Washington, D.C.: AFL-CIO, 1985), p. 31.

CASE 2
LEGISLATIVE STANDARDS FOR UNION OFFICES

Following are excerpts from the testimony of President Lane Kirkland, AFL-CIO, before the Labor-Management Relations Subcommittee of the House

Committee on Education and Labor, U.S. House of Representatives, December 12, 1982:

> S.1785, as we understand it, provides in essence as follows: First, that an employer payment to a union representative of $1,000 or more and the receipt of such a payment, now made unlawful by §302 of the Taft-Hartley Act, shall, where the violation is willful, henceforth be treated as a felony rather than a misdemeanor. Second, that the list of disqualifying crimes stated in the Landrum-Griffin Act and in Employment Retirement and Income Security Act (ERISA) shall be enlarged to include felonies that involve a breach of union or benefit fund trust. To use the proposed statutory language, conviction of a felony that "involves the misuse or abuse" of union or benefit fund office or employment would result in disqualification from union and benefit fund position. Third, that disqualification shall be as of the date of the trial court's judgment rather than as of the date that judgment becomes final with the proviso that an individual who appeals and prevails shall be paid his lost salary which has been held in escrow pending the appeal, and the disqualification lifted. Fourth, that the scope of disqualification shall be broadened to preclude the holding of any union or benefit fund position. And, fifth, that the period of disqualification—presently 5 years—shall be no less than 5 years and no more than 10 years.

Our canvass of the applicable law shows that the present Landrum-Griffin and ERISA disqualification provisions are substantially more stringent than those that apply to individuals who hold positions in other organizations. We accept with equanimity that evident inequality. The trade union movement's high purpose is to forward the best aspirations of working people.

Union office is a calling, not a business. The morals of the marketplace will not suffice. Those who enter that calling are, and should be, held to a higher standard. If a person holding union office takes an employer payoff for a substandard contract, misuses the right to strike for his own benefit or pilfers from the union treasury, that person does not simply stain his own honor. He tarnishes the bright efforts of the scores of men and women who have labored to create and maintain organizations worthy of the members who are privileged to represent and of society's good judgment. . . .

Passage of the Landrum-Griffin Act marked a new stage in the federal government's regulation of unions. That Act granted the Labor and Justice Departments far-reaching authority to supervise internal union affairs. Not only is the applicable federal criminal law wide-ranging, it has been vigorously enforced. Thousands of hours and millions of taxpayer dollars have been spent looking into every aspect of union affairs. The FBI, the Justice Department, the United States Attorneys, the Strike Forces and the Labor Department have pushed both the laws I have enumerated and the investigatory powers those laws created to their very extremes. That has been true in Democratic and Republican Administrations alike. . . .

We simply do not have the resources—the trained manpower, the subpoena, the grand jury, the authority to uncover and punish perjury, the due process trial procedures that settle with authority questions of innocence and guilt and the effective sanctions to punish the guilty. We have learned through hard experience that the allegations of criminal wrongdoing everyone supposes to be well founded do not always stand up when all the facts are brought out. We have also learned that occasionally the union officer one would unhesitantly vouch for can suddenly plead guilty to serious crime. Neither the adage that where there is smoke there is fire nor its converse—that where there is no smoke there is no fire—has proved a sound guide for our efforts at internal regulation. . . .

We are idealist enough to wish there was no such need, but we are realists enough to know that in an imperfect world there are occasions that call for use of the criminal law. One such occasion is corrupt action by union officers. . . .

By far the most problematic step S.1785 takes is to provide that disqualification from union or benefit fund office or employment takes effect on the trial court's judgment that the defendant is guilty of one of the enumerated crimes rather than after the appeals from that judgment have run their course. . . .

This is a hard rule; one which may be unjust in particular applications and which raises troubling civil liberties issues. The alternative, however, raises even more troubling questions for the continued good health of the trade union movement. Torn as we are between these concerns, we believe that our obligations to the membership and the integrity of our organizations must be put first. The sponsor's decision to provide that the convicted defendant's salary will be held in escrow and paid to him if his appeal succeeds does tend to alleviate the harshest consequences of this suggested change in the law.

Questions

1. Do you agree with the position President Kirkland urged? How do you compare this position with that of the Federation in 1940 (case 1)? How do you account for the differences?

2. Why should a union official be held to a higher standard on issues of corruption or financial malfeasance than a public official or a business executive?

3. Should issues of corruption or financial malfeasance be handled exclusively as a matter of internal union governance? What prevents them from being handled exclusively in that way?

4. In the evolution of the labor federation, the federal government has come to play a much larger role than it did in the 1880s. Describe the major changes. How do you account for these developments? How would you project the future role of government in such internal union affairs? Could governmental intervention have been avoided or constricted?

CASE 3
CARPENTER-MACHINIST DISPUTE

Probably the most extensive and intense jurisdictional dispute in the AFL for more than a half-century involved the United Brotherhood of Carpenters and Joiners of America and the International Association of Machinists over the work of machinery erection and installation. The shift from wooden machinery (pulleys, shafts, and belts) to metal machinery, the installation of equipment in the course of construction of plants, power generation stations and buildings in which a variety of construction contractors and building trades crafts were present, and the relative isolation of some sites from central cities tended to complicate the rivalry.

On numerous occasions from the early part of the century, the AFL conventions and the executive council rendered decisions in this dispute between these large and influential organizations. No decision was jointly accepted, and no mediation efforts or direct negotiations were successful, and for various years one organization or the other withdrew or was expelled from the Federation in protest of or noncompliance with the Federation's decision. For a period until 1915, when they were declared not to be building tradesmen, the Machinists were a member of the Building and Construction Trades Department (founded in 1908), and the department had also rendered decisions that were not accepted. Frank Duffy, general secretary of the Carpenters, stated the view: "We reserve the right to say what our jurisdiction claims shall cover, and we don't propose that they shall be curtailed, altered or amended through any other agency" (1916).

These disputes continued over the years despite some attempt at direct negotiations and legal proceeding. It was a dispute between the Carpenters and Machinists in the Anheuser-Busch Brewery in St. Louis that led to the

Supreme Court decision in *United States v. Hutcheson* (1941) that held that such conflict was not violative of the antitrust laws. In 1947, however, the Congress enacted section 8(b)(4)(D) and section 10(k) of the Taft-Hartley amendments that empowered the NLRB to decide such cases, and a number of cases involving these two organizations were referred to the board.

By the early 1950s new presidents had recently taken office in both organizations, and joint committees with outsider advisers or mediators [John T. Dunlop and Father William I. Kelley] were appointed to assist in a joint resolution of this long-standing dispute. An agreement ratified by both organizations on September 18, 1954, was administered by joint committees and applied to specific cases for a number of years. Although some issues have since arisen, the range of disputes is relatively minor and the past intensity of the dispute is gone. The agreement follows.

Agreement between the United Brotherhood of Carpenters and Joiners of America and the International Association of Machinists

This agreement is entered into between the International Association of Machinists and the United Brotherhood of Carpenters and Joiners of America for the purpose of improving relations between the two trades, facilitating the settlement of jurisdictional disputes directly between the two trades and establishing an understanding that will mutually assist each union to secure and to perform work coming within its recognized jurisdiction.

It is expressly understood and agreed that this agreement shall not relate to nor have any bearing on jurisdictional disputes that may exist or in the future occur between either of the parties hereto with any other International Union or subordinate body thereof.

Wherever the term "Millwright" is used in this agreement, it refers to members of the United Brotherhood of Carpenters and Joiners of America.

Article I

It is agreed that the International Association of Machinists has jurisdiction over the following work:

Section (a) The manufacturing, handling, erecting, installing and repairing of machinery and equipment except as provided in Articles II, III, and IV.

Section (b) The manufacturing, installing, erecting and repairing of printing presses of all kinds and auxiliary printing machinery.

Section (c) The handling, erecting and installing of the following brewery and bottling plant equipment: Fillers, crowners, double seamers and labelers along with that part of conveyor which is generally furnished with these machines by manufacturer thereof and recognized as a direct part of the machine.

Section (d) All machine shop work in connection with construction. This includes machine shops on construction sites and those servicing the project located away from the site.

Article II

It is agreed that the United Brotherhood of Carpenters and Joiners of America has jurisdiction over the following work:

Section (a) The handling, erecting and installing of machinery, motors, conveyors and equipment in new construction and additions, except as provided in Articles I, III, and IV.

Section (b) The handling, erecting and installing of the following brewery and bottling plant equipment: Washers, pasteurizers, packaging machines and all conveyors other than those referred to in Article I, Section (c).

Article III

In a plant or factory where the International Association of Machinists has been certified or recognized as the bargaining agent, or any plant where there is no such certification or recognition and Machinists are employed directly or through a contractor for the handling, erecting and installing of machinery and equipment, the United Brotherhood of Carpenters and Joiners of America shall not interfere with work covered by such certification, recognition or contract. In a plant or factory where the United Brotherhood of Carpenters and Joiners of America has been certified or recognized as the bargaining agent or any plant where there is no such certification or recognition and Millwrights are employed directly or through a contractor for handling, erecting and installing of machinery and equipment, the International Association of Machinists shall not interfere with work covered by such certification, recognition or contract. Where there is not past practice of either Machinists or Millwrights handling and installing machinery in existing buildings or plants, said work is recognized as coming under the jurisdiction of and shall be performed by Machinists. Where both organizations have been certified or recognized as the bargaining agent in the same plant, factory or project for certain groups of employees, this agreement shall not be used to alter the existing division of work between the employees of the two bargaining units.

Article IV

Section (a) The erection and installation of steam, hydro and gas turbines and generator units shall be performed by a composite crew of equal numbers of Machinists and Millwrights. Work shall be performed under the collective bargaining agreements or working rules of the Millwrights.*

Section (b) Foremen on steam and gas turbines and generator installations shall be Millwrights.† Foremen on hydro installations shall be Machinists. Foremen shall not be counted in the determination of a composite crew.

Section (c) The installation of auxiliary equipment in connection with power generating stations shall be performed by Millwrights.

Article V

Work in process on the date of this agreement shall be completed in accordance with the existing assignments.

Article VI

The parties hereto agree that no stoppage of work or any strike of its members, either collectively or individually, shall be entered into in any dispute in accordance with the following procedures:

(1) Should a dispute arise as to whether the members of one organization or the other should perform certain work, the local representatives of the two Unions shall endeavor to settle the dispute.

---

*Excerpt as provided for in the supplemental letters exchanged between the presidents of the two International Unions.
†Ibid.

(2) Should the local representatives fail to reach agreement, either representative may refer the dispute to the President of his International Union. The International President may communicate with the other International President, and both shall then assign International Representatives to meet within a week to settle the dispute.

(3) Should the representatives selected by the Presidents of the two International Unions be unable to reach a satisfactory agreement, they shall promptly prepare an accurate written description of the disputed work, jointly sign it, for submission to the two International Presidents. On the request of either International President, both shall each appoint a committee of not more than three members to meet within thirty days for the purpose of settling the dispute. If the joint committees fail to agree, on the request of either International President within thirty days, the dispute shall be submitted to final and binding arbitration before a neutral arbitrator selected under arrangements worked out by the two International Presidents.

Article VII

This agreement shall take effect September 18, 1954 and be in force for two year(s) during which time committees appointed by the Presidents of both International Unions shall jointly meet periodically to review work covered by this agreement and to consider new problems.

Unless notice of a desire to change or modify the agreement is served by one Union on the other sixty (60) days prior to its termination date, it shall automatically continue for another period of two year(s).

UNITED BROTHERHOOD OF CARPENTERS AND JOINERS OF AMERICA	INTERNATIONAL ASSOCIATION OF MACHINISTS
M.A. Hutcheson General President	A.J. Hayes International President
O.Wm. Blaier R.E. Roberts Raleigh Rajoppi	Eric Peterson P.L. Siemiller Elmer Walker
Committee	*Committee*
Approved by the General Executive Board September 18, 1954	Approved by the Executive Council September 18, 1954

Questions

1. Why was this dispute so difficult to resolve over the years? Would any other procedures than were tried have been successful in the context of the earlier era? Were such intense conflicts characteristic of labor movements of other countries?

2. What would you expect explains that in the agreement of September 18, 1954, the installation of printing machinery and machine shop work was assigned to machinists and the installation of equipment in brewery and bottling plants was assigned to carpenters (millwrights)?

3. What interests do contractors and industrial owners have in such an agreement and in the particular division of work? How does such a division of work affect costs and other policies of industrial managements and contractors and their competitive positions? How can the agreement survive if the NLRB provides different determinations in jurisdictional disputes? How can the agreement be made compatible with the law?

4. How stable is such an agreement? What factors will operate to affect its longevity and its adaptability to changes in technology, markets, and organizational patterns of local unions?

5. What administrative arrangements should be established to settle differences between local unions and industrial managements and contractors over the interpretation of the agreement? over new types of work?

CASE 4
LIMITS TO THE NO-RAIDING
CONSTITUTIONAL OBLIGATION

Article XX of the constitution of the AFL-CIO provides in part as follows:

Section 2. Each affiliate shall respect the established collective bargaining relationship of every other affiliate. No affiliate shall organize or attempt to represent employees as to whom an established collective bargaining relationship exists with any other affiliate. For purposes of this Article, the term, "established collective bargaining relationship" means any situation in which an affiliate, or any local or other subordinate body thereof, has either (a) been recognized by the employer (including any governmental agency) as the collective bargaining representative for the employees involved for a period of one year or more, or (b) been certified by the National Labor Relations Board or other federal or state agency as the collective bargaining representative for the employees.

The International Union of Electrical Radio and Machine Workers (IUE) is charged by the Distillery, Rectifying, Wine and Allied Workers International Union of America with violation of this section of the constitution.

IUE contends that it is not in violation as charged because of several facts. First, the Distillery Workers placed Local 39 in trusteeship on October 23, 1969, and the employees have been without service from their union ever since, particularly having had no grievances processed during this period. Second, the Distillery Workers and its Local 39 were decertified on September 2, 1971, in proceedings conducted by the NLRB. Third, IUE did not seek out these employees; it was sought out by them with the request that they be permitted to become affiliated with the IUE.

While this may be immaterial, it should be explained that the trusteeship grew out of action by Local 39, against the instructions of the IUE and contrary to the no-strike provision of their contract, to support the strike action of another union that was in disagreement with a subsidiary of Brown-Forman Distillers.

Questions

1. How would you decide this case?
2. Does decertification of a bargaining representation by the NLRB or a state agency create a circumstance in which another union in the Federation may properly seek to represent the workers?
3. May a union seek to set aside a certified representation if it can show that the representative has not serviced the workers, has substandard agreements, or has not handled grievances of workers? If a union within the Federation is not allowed to intervene in such cases, may not membership be lost to nonaffiliated unions?
4. How do you assess the proposition that competition among unions is an essential condition for growth in membership and a vigorous labor movement? Is competition among unions compatible with no raiding?
5. How should this situation be handled, in your view, by the IUE? What should the members of the Distillery Workers who approached the IUE be told?
6. In what respects does the AFL-CIO constitution simply conform to the law in regulating competition among union affiliates for members, certification, employer recognition, and work opportunities, and in what specific respects do these constitutional restraints exceed those of the public law?

CASE 5
CIO ORGANIZATIONAL DISPUTES AGREEMENT

The United Auto Workers (UAW) and the United Glass and Ceramic Workers (UGW), both CIO affiliates, were in competition to organize a new glass plant to produce automobile glass for the Ford Motor Company. Which union would better serve the interests of the employees involved?

In July 1955, the Ford Motor Company announced plans for the construction of a new glass production plant to be located at Nashville, Tennessee. Following this announcement and prior to the completion of the plant, both UAW and UGW asserted jurisdiction. When negotiations failed to resolve the dispute, the problem was referred to arbitration under the Organizational Disputes Agreement.

The announced plans for the Nashville plant indicate that it is to be devoted exclusively to the manufacture of glass parts such as windshields, side windows, and rear windows, which are to be made to the specifications of the Ford Motor Company and will be usable only on cars manufactured by that company. The finished windshields and windows are to be shipped to Ford Assembly Plants for installation. The employment of the full working force of approximately 2,200 employees is expected to be completed during spring 1957.

Position of UGW

As its first major point, the UGW argues that its charter covers jurisdiction of the flat glass industry and that its charter application included, among other items, specific reference to glass used in automobiles. This charter was granted by the AFL in 1934 to their organization, which was then called the Flat Glass Workers of America. The UGW points out that subsequent change in its name, the expansion of its jurisdiction to include related workers, and its affiliation with the CIO did not in any way affect or modify its original jurisdiction over flat glass.

As a second major point, the UGW points out that it has organized, with only three exceptions, all plants manufacturing flat glass. These three exceptions are the two Ford glass plants at St. Paul, Minnesota, and Dearborn, Michigan, which are organized by UAW, and the Blackford Glass Company at Vincennes, Indiana, in which the independent union is negotiating for a merger with the UGW.

The UGW argues that the reasons that led to the organization of the two Ford glass plants in 1941 by UAW do not apply to the new Nashville plant.

UGW gives this account to explain why the two Ford plants were organized by UAW. In 1937, when the plants were unorganized, the UGW was in poor organizational and financial shape, and an administrator had been appointed by John L. Lewis, then president of the CIO, to administer its affairs. The administrator applied for financial assistance in organizing the Ford glass production plants but was refused because the available funds were urgently needed elsewhere. In 1941, the peak of the CIO organizational drive at the Ford Motor Company, top CIO officers decided that the policy would be to organize Ford into one unit and argue jurisdiction later. UGW further argues (1) that now UGW has ample funds for efficient organization; (2) the new plant is a separate glass factory and not integrated with the assembly and production lines as was the case at St. Paul and Dearborn; (3) the glass from the new Ford plant will supplement present production by Ford and will replace glass now being purchased from other plants where the employees are under contract with UGW; and (4) the inclusion of the Ford plant at Nashville in UGW is important to the maintaining of wage standards in the glass industry.

With respect to its organizational capabilities in the area, UGW points out that within a 225-mile radius of Nashville, it has contracts in thirteen plants; it maintains a regional office at St. Louis, Missouri, and a subregional office at Knoxville, Tennessee. The UGW states that if given organizational rights at the Nashville plant, it intends to open a subregional office at Nashville.

The UGW further argues that since the sole product of the plant will be flat glass, the problems of the employees will be tied in with the peculiar economics of the flat glass industry and can be effectively dealt with only by a union set up in the flat glass industry on an industry-wide basis. The UGW further points to the fact that glass workers have a high average hourly rate of pay, higher than the average hourly earnings of automobile workers.

Position of UAW

In support of its claim for organizational rights at the Nashville plant, UAW argues that it would be to the best interests of the employees at Nashville to be represented by the same union that represents 99 percent of the other employees of the Ford Motor Company. This claim of UAW is based on two arguments.

The first argument runs as follows: UAW already represents the employees at the existing glass plants within the Ford Motor Company at Dearborn and St. Paul; that the projected Nashville plant is merely an extension of the Dearborn and St. Paul plants, and that it therefore would be in the best interest of the employees at Nashville to be represented by the same union, which already represents the employees engaged in the production of glass in the other Ford Motor Company plants.

The second argument is that the Nashville plant will be closely integrated with existing glass production facilities from the standpoint of both production and management, including industrial relations policy. UAW points out that the Nashville plant is to produce glass to be used exclusively in cars produced by the Ford Motor Company and that the three plants will produce less than 50 percent of Ford's current glass requirements. The UAW points out that the Ford Company plans to transfer certain operations now performed at Dearborn to Nashville and that certain types of glass made at the Nashville plant will be shipped to the Dearborn plant for the finishing processes; the machinery and the methods to be used in both plants will be similar; it is contemplated that the Nashville and Dearborn plants will cover for each other in periods of breakdowns, emergencies, or major repairs; and finally, production at the three plants will be tied in closely with the vehicle production schedules of the entire Ford Motor Company. On the basis of this integration of production and management, the UAW argues that the employees at Nashville will benefit more by being represented by the union that now represents the employees at all other Ford glass plants.

The UAW also claims to have charter rights to organize the Nashville plant. In that connection, it points out, first, that the plant will manufacture only automobile parts—windshield and window lights—and therefore properly falls within the charter and customary jurisdiction of the UAW; and second, that two-thirds of all Ford employees are engaged in the production of parts rather than in the assembly of parts into completed vehicles.

With regard to national and area organization and its ability to serve the employees at Nashville, the UAW makes the following points:

1. In the immediate area of the Nashville plant, there are three major and two minor Ford facilities employing 6,000 workers who are members of the UAW; that within an area of a 225-mile radius from Nashville there are 25,000 members of the UAW who are served by a regional office and three subregional offices, employing a total of fifteen full-time representatives.

2. The UAW has successfully organized the greater part of the automobile and the automotive parts industries, and in the Ford Company in particular it has organized in excess of 99 percent of all production and maintenance employees.

3. If UAW is granted jurisdiction in this plant, the employees would automatically come under the national Ford contract, and the employees would become a part of the 140,000 Ford employees now represented by UAW in Ford.

4. Under this contract the employees would be assured of the basic Ford wages, together with substantial fringe benefits, as well as the services and facilities of the Ford Department of the UAW.

Basis for Decision

The Organizational Disputes Agreement in Paragraph 5(c) sets forth the criteria established for the guidance of the Organizational Disputes Arbitrator. Paragraph 5(c) reads:

c. In deciding which union is the appropriate union to conduct an organizing campaign, he shall make his determination on the basis of what will best serve the interests of the employees involved and will preserve the good name and orderly functioning of the C.I.O., and shall give due consideration to all of the relevant facts and circumstances including the following factors where he deems them relevant:

The charter or customary jurisdiction of each of the unions involved.

The extent to which each of the unions involved have organized:
a. the industry,
b. the area,
c. the particular plant involved,

The ability of each of the unions to provide service to the employees involved.[1]

Questions

1. What decision would you make in this case? Develop the basis for the decision.
2. Was the organizational disputes arbitrator confronted with an issue of jurisdiction? exclusive jurisdiction or organizing jurisdiction?
3. Should the views and preferences of the company enter into the determination? If so, through what process? Should the employer be invited to a hearing?
4. What were the reasons for the plan to eliminate all but one CIO union to compete for representation on an NLRB ballot? Would a similar plan, adopted in 1986, increase the representation results of AFL-CIO unions today?
5. What are the consequences for collective bargaining and for the competitiveness of business establishments and the economic status of their

workers that follow from the elimination of the principle of exclusive representation and the introduction of established bargaining relationships as the basic constitutional principle? Does not multiple representation within a group of competing establishments create special problems for both businesses and their workers and their unions in collective bargaining? Is coalition bargaining an effective resolution of these difficulties?

6. What enforcement mechanism is available to support a decision? What policy should the NLRB follow toward such a private procedure?

Note

1. AFL-CIO, Industrial Union Department, *The Organizational Disputes Agreement, Decisions of the Arbitrator, 1951–57,* Decision No. 31, pp. 175–182. (David H. Stowe, Organizational Disputes Arbitrator).

CASE 6
AFL-CIO ORGANIZING RESPONSIBILITY PROCEDURES

One of the cases to arise under the Procedures for Determining Organizing Responsibilities of the AFL-CIO, adopted by the executive council in 1986 and subsequently in Article XXI of the constitution, concerned Adolph Coors Company, Brewing Division, in Golden, Colorado. Both the Machinists and the Teamsters had sought to organize the production and maintenance unit of employees in this brewery, which had been the focus of a long history of conflict between Coors and the Federation. The brand had been placed on the "unfair" list and made the object of a nationwide union boycott.

It is to be recalled that the International Brotherhood of Teamsters, Chauffeurs, Warehousemen and Helpers had been expelled in 1957 by the AFL-CIO on grounds of corruption. Their application for readmission into the Federation was accepted in 1987 on the explicit understanding that they would comply with the constitution, including Articles XX and XXI.

The Teamsters initiated the procedures for determining organizing responsibility at the Golden, Colorado, brewery. They sought a determination under Article XXI to become the exclusive representative of these employees "without being subject to ongoing competition by another AFL-CIO affiliate" (section 2). Mediation proved unsuccessful, and an umpire, Murray Finley, retired president of the Amalgamated Clothing and Textile Workers Union, heard the dispute between the Machinists and the Teamsters on March 23,

1988, and issued a decision a week later. The decision contains the following three paragraphs:

I was greatly assisted in my thinking by the fact that the Teamsters and the Machinists agreed on three critical points: that the Teamsters' organizing effort began before the Machinists'; that the present organizing competition between the Teamsters and the Machinists makes it all but impossible for either one to succeed in securing a majority vote at Coors' Golden, Colorado facility in the event that both unions are on a representation election ballot; and that because the Golden brewery is so much larger and so much better established than the Elkton, Virginia facility it is likely that the Elkton employees will follow the lead of the Golden employees rather than the other way around.

In light of these points of agreement I proceeded by comparing the Teamsters' and Machinists' organizing efforts at Coors' Golden, Colorado facility according to the factors stated in paragraph 6 of the AFL-CIO Executive Council's February 19, 1988 Statement on Implementing Article XXI of the AFL-CIO Constitution (see below), taking each of those factors one by one and then weighing all the factors together in order to determine the likelihood of an organizing success.

After going through that process, I am firmly convinced that as impressive as the Machinists' effort has been, on every count, the Teamsters' program is significantly stronger. I believe, as well, that the Teamsters have an excellent chance of successfully organizing the employees at Coors' Golden, Colorado facility. While no one fact was decisive it does appear to me that the Teamsters' recent accomplishments in securing recognition—and an extremely favorable collective bargaining agreement—at the new Anheuser-Busch brewery in Ft. Collins, Colorado gives IBT's organizing campaign in Golden—which is only 50 miles away—significant added impetus. Given the very different organizing strategies the Teamsters and Machinists are following I wish to emphasize that I have made every effort to judge this matter on the particular facts before me and not according to my subjective views of sound organizing procedures. (Indeed, while my award is basically in favor of the Teamsters, as a general proposition I see a good deal of merit in the Machinists' approach which incorporates a number of innovative techniques that my own union has helped to develop.)

The factors specified in paragraph 6 of the February 19, 1988, statement of the AFL-CIO executive council referred to by the umpire are as follows:

(a) current support among the employee group;

(b) support from the affiliates pursuant to a coordinated organizing campaign and the auspices of the AFL-CIO or a trade or industrial department;

(c) the extent and effectiveness of recent organizing activity with respect to the same employer, the same industry, employment sector or occupational categories and/or the same geographic area;

(d) resources already expended, budgeted or projected to be expended on the organizing and collective bargaining;

(e) existing membership employed by, and bargaining relationships with, the same employer;

(f) membership strength in the geographic area;

(g) the number and/or percentage of current members within the industry and/or the occupational categories being organized.

Questions

1. Article XXI begins by stating that in order to resolve organizing competition in those situations in which the competition may be detrimental to the best interest of the workers involved and the trade union movement, the federation shall maintain a procedure for determining organizing responsibilities. Do you think there has been too much or too little competition for members or work opportunities in the labor movement?

2. Is competition an impediment or stimulus to union growth? The period of early conflict between the AFL and the CIO was also a period of rapid growth. How much competition, and in what forms, is appropriate in the labor movement?

3. Assess the standards specified for the umpire in deciding among competing affiliates of the AFL-CIO. What weight would you assign to the capacity of an affiliate to service members as compared to the likely success in organizing an employee group?

4. How do you evaluate the problem of getting employees who have indicated a preference for one union, by signing an authorization card, to shift allegiance to another union that received the award of the umpire to achieve a majority vote for an affiliated union? How would you feel with the problem as a winner or loser?

5. How would you design a way to reach a conclusion as to whether the mechanism for resolving organizing disputes among affiliated unions, Article XXI, was successful? How would you estimate the savings in organizing dollars and time made possible by the procedures for resolving organizing disputes?

5
National Unions and Local Unions

National unions originally were the creation of isolated local unions and their leaders in the same craft or industry drawn together from different parts of the country. For instance, the National Union of Ironmolders was formed in 1859 at the convention held in Philadelphia with thirty-five delegates representing unions from twelve cities; the United Brotherhood of Carpenters and Joiners held its first convention in Chicago in 1881 with thirty-six delegates from eleven cities representing 4,800 members. As national unions were established, they organized new local unions, nurtured the growth of existing local unions, and provided services to them and to their members.

Federations have on occasions issued charters to a national union without significant affiliation of local unions or members for the purpose of encouraging the formation of new local unions in a sector and the attraction of new members. A number of national unions were formed in this way, largely from the top down, during the period of intense rivalry between the AFL and the CIO from 1935 to 1955.

Early Developments

Among the early national unions with a continuous existence to this day are the International Molders' and Allied Workers' Union (1859), Brotherhood of Locomotive Engineers (1863), International Union of Bricklayers and Allied Craftsmen (1865), National Marine Engineers' Beneficial Association (1875), United Brotherhood of Carpenters and Joiners of America (1881), and the United Mineworkers of America (1890). Such national unions, and those that have merged or expired, in their early constitutions and in their experience with local unions and members provided lessons and alternative patterns for later emerging national unions. The early unions were also influenced by the practices and perspectives of labor organizations in various countries of Europe, particularly Great Britain, from which many workers

Table 5–1
Increase of American National Trade Unions, 1850–1940

Period	Total Formed	Total Disappeared	Total in Existence at End of Decade
1850–1859	6	0	6
1860–1869	24	1	29
1870–1879	20	20	29
1880–1889	62	12	79
1890–1899	77	26	120
1900–1909	95	44	131
1910–1919	34	42	163
1920–1929	17	28	152
1930–1939	66	24	194

Source: Lloyd Ulman, *The Rise of the National Union* (Cambridge: Harvard University Press, 1955), p. 4.

had emigrated. But probably most of all, the emerging national unions were influenced by the pragmatic experience in their industrial and community environments of grappling with problems of governance and the necessity of maintaining the support of members in the face of hostile employers and a largely uncongenial legal setting.

The significance of the early national unions to the future governance of labor organizations can be better understood by examining table 5–1, which shows the rate of formation and disappearance of national unions by decades. The 1880s and 1890s and the first decade of this century were the era of the greatest emergence of national unions. (The 1930s with the CIO and AFL rivalry was also a period of rapid expansion in the number of national unions.) The early unions often were to provide the precedents, the experience, and the influence by example to shape later developments or at least to reveal options and issues to national unions established later.[1]

The early national unions perforce had to experiment with various procedures, constitutional provisions, and devices of governance in their particular setting and with the characteristics of their members and the work force they sought to attract. These early processes by trial and error encompassed all of the complexities of internal union government.

A number of issues were vital to shaping the government of the developing national unions. These factors were uninfluenced by explicit government regulatory prescriptions as incorporated in the 1959 Landrum-Griffin statute.

Site of National Office

In many of the early national unions, the office was moved with the address of the annually elected president. A fixed headquarters required a full-time paid president or a paid secretary-treasurer that many unions could not afford at the outset. The location of headquarters near an influential local union caused many problems because that local might seek to exert undue influence over the emerging national union.

At one time many national union headquarters were located in Indianapolis, a juncture of railroads going east and west. In the past generation, Washington, D.C., has become the location of the headquarters of the largest number of national unions, recognizing the signal influences of national governmental activities.

Term and Turnover in the Principal Office

At their outset many national unions provided for an annual term for officers, and the principal officers were changed annually or at short intervals. The rotation of headquarters and officers was symbolic of the control of the national office by the strongest locals. As longer terms and longer tenure in office developed, the roles of national unions relative to local unions were strengthened. Further, the national unions generally developed the custom of making the president the principal executive officer rather than the secretary serving that role, as was the case in British unions. In a few national unions in the United States, however, including the Butcher Workers, the secretary was the principal officer.

Election of Officers

This early issue—whether to elect by convention or by referendum of all workers—remains an active question, or has had a renascence, in some national unions (including the Mineworkers and dissidents in the Teamsters).

In most national unions, elected convention delegates elect national officers. The process of selection of officers is a part of the larger question of the relative roles in policy decisions of elected convention delegates and initiative and referenda votes by the membership as a whole. In the late years of the nineteenth century and early years of the twentieth century, as in the body politic of the country, many national unions experimented extensively with direct voting of members on a wide range of policy issues. They debated intensely as to which procedure was more democratic or produced the wisest decisions for the organization. The verdict of their experience in most unions tended to be for convention decisions on the grounds that many members did not vote and that representative conventions had the merit of direct debate and compromise, including carrying the examination of difficult issues over from one convention to another.

Expenses for Convention Delegates

Various national unions experimented with various means to ensure attendance at conventions. Small local unions and those in remote areas were often disadvantaged, in comparison with larger locals, by not having the financial resources to pay the expenses of delegates. Many small locals simply did not send delegates. This issue was more significant in some national unions with many small locals compared to other national unions with large locals reflecting employment patterns. If national unions were to pay expenses of delegates to conventions, how should these funds be raised? Such funding would influence the frequency of conventions. Practices on this matter have varied widely among national unions.

Apprenticeship Standards

In unions of skilled trades with apprenticeship programs, such as Printers, Molders, Bricklayers, and Machinists, divergent apprenticeship standards, ratios, and years of training among isolated local unions became a matter of concern, helping to develop the institution of the national union with standardized apprenticeship. Members of local unions in one community traveled to other localities, and employers with different standards and apprenticeship ratios competed with each other.

Traveling Members

The various problems created by traveling members from one locality to another in many unions was a decisive impetus to the development of national union policies and governance. As the national transportation system and markets after the Civil War developed in the United States, the mobility and competition among workers grew. Isolated local unions were confronted with issues of how to identify and what to do with scabs or strikebreakers who moved from one community to another. Employers often advertised in other communities to recruit labor to fill vacancies or to take the place of strikers. Many national unions developed a traveling card system. Professor Ulman has concluded, "For purposes of discipline, the traveling member had to be regarded as a citizen of the national union rather than merely as a member of one particular local union, be it the local of origin or the local of destination.[2]

Internal Discipline and Trials

National unions were early confronted with the task of providing for a form of an internal judicial system, specifying crimes against the union organization, procedures for the trial of individual members or local or national leaders or subordinate bodies, and for an internal appellate procedure. In recent years a few national unions, such as the UAW, have established a public review board, comprised of outside neutrals, to hear and decide grievances against the actions of the national union.

Assistance in Negotiations

In a number of industries, isolated local unions were confronted in negotiations with employers that had plants or operations in more than one locality or employers who moved from one locality to another. The growth of markets facilitated by the transportation system and financial institutions enhanced these developments, as John R. Commons long ago explained. It was essential for the locals to have reliable information and assistance in dealing with a common opponent. The national union was to provide such coordination and to facilitate strategic selection of negotiations and strike with the assistance of a national strike fund. The experience of national union leaders often also provided perspective and responsibility that facilitated settlement in negotiations. As areas of market competition increased in some industries, the role of national unions in negotiations was strengthened.

Strike Benefits

The national union provided the opportunity to focus a strike, or to resist a lockout, at one point in an industry and to support those out of work by strike benefits. The issue often arose in the early years as to whether strike fund resources should be left with local unions or concentrated in the hands of the national union. In time, the payment of strike benefits carried with it the necessity that the national union approve the strike if any benefits were to be paid. The approval of a strike per se was a separate decision.

Dues and Assessments

The financing of a national union and its activities by dues and assessments on the members of local unions is a persistent issue in the governance of national unions. Taxation is as sensitive an issue in union government as in the general polity. Some unions have sought to avoid repeated requests for higher dues levels with general inflation by specifying dues as a percentage of the negotiated wage scales. Most national unions collect revenue from local unions as a per capita payment per member, as an authorized assessment, and as a share of initiation fees. In the Steelworkers, by contrast, the checkoff of dues by employers is paid directly to the national union, and a share is remitted by the national union to the appropriate local union.

Actions by Public Agencies

Isolated local unions believed that one of the purposes of a national organization was to promote legislation or influence administrative action of governments in their interests and to redress problems they could not confront so effectively alone or through collective bargaining. The interests of the maritime trades in legislation for safety at sea, the concern of the Carpenters to "abolish the use of convict labor to produce competitive goods," and the devotion of the coal miners to mine safety and mine inspection legislation are illustrative of these influences in particular environments shaping national labor organizations. The activities of national unions in these directions in turn shaped internal organization, design, and staff, creating a specialized staff and Washington bent.

The emerging and developing national unions of the nineteenth and early twentieth centuries grappled with the sorts of issues outlined and experimented with various policies and procedures, each in the setting of its competitive markets and the purposes of its members. National union governance thus evolved slowly over the years with a great deal of response to trial and error in changing circumstances.

National Union Organizers and Representatives

The early national unions were instrumental in creating the position of traveling organizers from which emerged today's national union representative. As their organizations grew, full-time national union officers, presidents, and secretary-treasurers could not well respond to all requests for assistance or organization in a growing country. In 1878 the Molders authorized its president and executive board to send out one or more organizers and to see "that every locality capable of maintaining a Union is attended to, and a thorough and systematic effort be made to organize them."[3] Some early organizers were compensated on the basis of the number of members they recruited. For the first time in 1899 the Federation employed a number of full-time paid organizers. In that year it spent $6,373.66 on organizing expenses—17.3 percent of its income, including assessments.[4]

The emergence of national union representatives assisting in the negotiation of collective agreements, settling strikes, investigating local union internal conflicts, and resolving disputes with other unions was an important innovation, influencing the relations between national unions and local unions. In a sense the national representative became an extension of the president and secretary-treasurer of the national union. These representatives tended to strengthen the influence and the authority of the national union. In most cases these representatives were appointed by the executives; in a few cases, such as the Plumbers and Steamfitters, they are elected like other national union officers.

These representatives perform a wide range of functions under the supervision of the elected president, vice-presidents, or other designated officers. They are part of the bureaucracy of the national union, facilitating the full range of activities of the national union.

Landrum-Griffin and Fair Representation

As national unions developed in the 1930s and 1940s, their internal governance and their relations with local unions continued largely to reflect their own experience and internal political processes, except for occasional court cases largely affecting due process and procedures. The enactment of the Landrum-Griffin Labor-Management Reporting and Disclosure Act (1959) following the McClellan committee hearings was designed to regulate a number of features of internal union governance. In an important sense this legislation was an unforeseen natural sequence to the Wagner Act (1935) and the Taft-Hartley Act (1947). A union could not expect to enjoy the rights conferred by government of exclusive representation, with an obligation on management to bargain in good faith with the union for all employees in the unit regardless of whether they were union members, and not expect the public to require certain standards of union conduct and governance.

The principal provisions of the statute concern a bill of rights of members, reporting by labor organizations and employers, trusteeships and supervision of local unions, and subordinate bodies and elections. These statutory regulations, and their interpretation by the Labor Department and the courts, have reshaped in some respects the constitutions developed historically by the national unions up to 1959.

The regulatory provisions have similarly enhanced materially the extent of litigation affecting internal union governance. Moreover, independent of the Landrum-Griffin statute, the courts developed the doctrine of fair representation respecting the rights of a minority group or an individual in a labor organization. The NLRB has adopted and in a number of ways extended the doctrine that is designed to prevent hostile discrimination of a minority by the labor organization or its officers.

Notes

1. For the classic discussion of the evolution of national unions, see Lloyd Ulman, *The Rise of the National Union* (Cambridge: Harvard University Press, 1955).

2. Ibid., p. 108.
3. Ibid., p. 227.
4. Philip Taft, *The AF of L in the Time of Gompers* (New York: Harper and Brothers, 1957), pp. 99–100.

Suggested Reading

David Brody, *The Butcher Workmen: A Study of Organization* (Cambridge: Harvard University Press, 1964).

H. A. Clegg, *The System of Industrial Relations in Great Britain* (Oxford: Basil Blackwell, 1970), pp. 1–118.

Jonathan Grossman, *William Sylvis, Pioneer of American Labor* (New York: Columbia University Press, 1945).

F. Ray Marshall, *Labor in the South* (Cambridge: Harvard University Press, 1967).

Martin Segal, *The Rise of the United Association: National Unionism in the Pipe Trades, 1884–1924* (Cambridge: Harvard University Press, 1970).

Philip Taft, *The Structure and Government of Labor Unions* (Cambridge: Harvard University Press, 1954).

Lloyd Ulman, *The Rise of the National Union: The Development and Significance of the Structure, Governing Institutions, and Economic Policies* (Cambridge: Harvard University Press, 1955).

CASE 1
AFFILIATION OF AN INDEPENDENT UNIT

An independent union of bank employees, the Firstbank Independent Employees Association, which had been certified by the NLRB, voted to affiliate with Local 1182 of the United Food and Commercial Workers International Union, AFL-CIO. Local 1182 was comprised of Retail Clerks.

In accordance with the independent union's constitution, only union members voted in the election to determine whether the organization favored the affiliation. Nonmember employees in the certified bargaining unit were not afforded an opportunity to vote on the affiliation question. The vote for affiliation was 1,206 in favor to 774 opposed.

In 1979 the NLRB determined that the affiliation did not substantially change the character of the union and amended the independent union's certification as the exclusive bargaining representative of the bank's employees to designate the newly affiliated union as the independent successor.[1]

The employer, Seattle-First National Bank, refused to bargain with the newly affiliated union. The NLRB then found the bank guilty of an unfair labor practice and ordered it to bargain (1979). The employer refused to comply and the issue entered the federal courts.

Because another case raised similar issues, the NLRB asked to have the case remanded to it from the courts, and that request was granted (1980). In 1982 the NLRB changed its earlier opinion and, by a three-to-two vote, concluded that excluding nonmembers from voting in affiliation decisions violates "fundamental due process standards."[2] The board revoked the newly affiliated union's amended certification and dismissed the previously granted refusal to bargain unfair labor practice charge against the bank.

This new rule of the board appeared to mean that an employer may, with impunity, refuse to bargain with any union that affiliates without permitting nonmember employees in the bargaining units to participate in what until recently was considered an internal union affair. "In effect, the Board now requires that *all* union affiliation decisions be put to a vote of all employees, union and non-union in the bargaining unit."

"The Board changed the rule because it now believes that affiliation is not an internal union matter. Instead, the Board suggests that affiliation by its very nature implicates the guaranteed rights of all employees to a bargaining representative selected by the majority. Under the Board's new approach, an affiliation decision will always call a union's continuing majority status into question."

The NLRB's new policy in 1982 required that nonunion employees be permitted to vote in union elections whether to affiliate with another union. This policy issue was taken by the union to the courts, and in 1986 the Supreme Court unanimously overturned the NLRB 1982 policy, restoring the old policy, which resulted in the certification of the union.[3]

The Court said, "The Board's rule effectively gives the employer the power to veto an independent union's decision to affiliate, thereby allowing the employer to directly interfere with union decision making Congress intended to insulate from outside interference." In the Court's view the NLRB had exceeded its statutory authority in adopting the new rule.

Questions

1. What interest is it of an employer whether a union is unaffiliated or affiliated with one or another national union? Is it appropriately any of the management's concern? What public interest, if any, is there in the matter of affiliation?

2. What rules should apply to an affiliation election? Who should conduct the election? Are NLRB election rules, internal union election rules, or rules common in public elections to apply to affiliation votes? What interest has an employer in the way in which such an election is conducted? How may an employer express such an interest?

3. What interests do nonmembers in a certified bargaining representative have in the issue of affiliation? If the nonmembers, for whom the union is obligated under the duty of fair representation, vote in a private affiliation election, what is likely to be their major concern? Are the prospects of a subsequent decertification election adequate protection for nonmembers in an affiliation vote?

4. It has often been said that a long-standing federal labor policy is to avoid unnecessary interference in internal union affairs. This view holds that there should be strong countervailing justification for interference. State the justification for such interference in cases of affiliation. The 1982 board appeared to hold that any affiliation constitutes a sufficient change in the character of the union to call the initial employee choice of bargaining representative into question. The board seemed to hold that affiliations are never simply an internal union affair. What is your view?

5. How should issues of policy, as illustrated in this case, or changes in such policy be resolved in industrial relations arrangements? Should the matter be decided by Congress? the courts? the Labor Department? the NLRB? without government interference? How would you propose to handle employer refusals to recognize a newly affiliated unit previously certified? Would you permit a strike and declare such a strike to be legal? How should such issues be handled for government employee units?

6. From the simple requirement of the Wagner Act for an election, certification and recognition by an employer is created—in this case, an opportunity for further government regulation of internal affairs of labor organizations. Can you give other illustrations?

7. How can the time delays in NLRB and court proceedings be more reasonably contained? What do you suppose went on in this bank for seven years after the vote for affiliation?

8. What are consequences for labor policy of the decision process with its long delays illustrated by this case? What can be done to redress such delays and such changes reflecting short-run considerations?

Notes

1. *Seattle-First National Bank*, 241 NLRB 751.
2. *Seattle-First National Bank*, 265 NLRB, no. 55, November 18, 1982.
3. *Seattle-First National Bank v. Financial Institution Employees of America*, 106 S. Ct. 1007 (1986).

CASE 2
QUALIFICATION FOR UNION OFFICE
AND VOTING

The Sailors' Union of the Pacific, an affiliate with 3,000 members of the Seafarers' International Union of North America, AFL-CIO, conducted an election of officers of the union from December 1, 1981, to January 31, 1982, in accordance with the union's constitution. Only individuals who had been union members for three years or more were eligible to run for office or to vote.

Peter Turner, a union member, filed a protest with the union president, and subsequently he filed a protest with the secretary of labor under section 402(a) of the Labor-Management Reporting and Disclosure Act of 1959. The secretary filed suit in the federal district court under the act to challenge the union's voting and candidate eligibility requirements and the election results. Section 401(e) of the act states in part:

In any election required by this section which is held by secret ballot a reasonable opportunity shall be given for the nomination of candidates and every member in good standing shall be eligible to be a candidate and to hold office (subject to . . . reasonable qualifications uniformly imposed) and shall have the right to vote for or otherwise support the candidate or candidates of his choice, without being subject to penalty, discipline, or improper interference or reprisal of any kind by such organization or any member thereof.

Section 404(b) of the act provides with respect to a complaint filed under section 401(a) with the secretary of labor that:

(b) The Secretary shall investigate such complaint and, if he finds probable cause to believe that a violation of this title has occurred and has not been remedied, he shall, within sixty days after the filing of such complaint, bring a civil action against the labor organization as an entity in the district court of the United States in which such labor organization maintains its principal office to set aside the invalid election, if any, and to direct the conduct of an election or hearing and vote upon the removal of officers under the supervision of the Secretary and in accordance with the provisions of this title and such rules and regulations as the Secretary may prescribe.

Under the regulations issued by the secretary of labor (29 C.F.R. 452.37) a union may limit candidate eligibility to those individuals who have been union members for at least two years, but a longer period is impermissible.

The secretary's regulations (29 C.F.R. 452.88) also provide that a union may reasonably require a new member to remain in good standing for up to a year before being permitted to vote, but a longer period is unreasonable. These regulations are not necessarily binding on the courts.

The Sailors' Union of the Pacific had recently passed the three-year rule in a constitutional referendum and in the view of the union is a clear indicator of the members' wishes.

It may be noted that the Supreme Court has ruled in several cases involving the reasonableness of candidate eligibility requirements in union elections. In a Steelworkers case, the Court held unreasonable a union rule limiting eligibility to members who had attended at least half the local's regular meetings for three years prior to the election.[1] The Court also invalidated a union rule that limited eligibility for major elective offices to members holding elective office or who had previously held elective office.[2]

The issue is to balance the free choice of candidates and eligibility to vote with the organization's interests in qualified and experienced officers. How narrow or broad a reach should be given to the "reasonable qualifications" provision of section 401(e) of the statute? Is it appropriate to have a uniform rule to cover all occupations and work environments?

Questions

1. In the maritime industry, workers are often away from port for long periods; they may come to know those on board one ship but do not have the opportunity to get acquainted or become known by all workers, as do those working at a fixed location. Do you think this argument is sufficient to support a three-year eligibility rule for union office or for eligibility to vote?

2. The secretary's regulations prescribe a uniform standard. Since industries and labor organizations vary enormously, what is the case for uniform regulations?

3. Why should a labor organization seek to place any restriction on eligibility of a member to run for union office or to vote in a union election? Consider the wide differences among unions and their work environments.

4. What basis or justification is there for the regulations issued by the secretary of labor? Where did these regulations come from? Are they not inherently arbitrary? How significant to anyone is the difference between three years and two years for eligibility for office and three years and one year for voters? Can anyone demonstrate an overwhelming public inter-

est in two years as compared to three years for eligibility to run for office in the maritime industry setting?

5. What would have been the consequences for the evolution of union government, sketched at the outset of this chapter, if statutory and administrative regulations of the type illustrated in this case had been in effect over the past hundred years? Do the statutory and administration regulations unduly inhibit experimentation and evolution in union governance? In what ways?

Notes

1. *Local 3489, United Steelworkers of America v. Usery,* 429 U.S. 305 (1977).
2. *Wirtz v. Hotel, Motel and Club Employees Union, Local 6,* 391 U.S. 492 (1968).

CASE 3
INTERNATIONAL UNION STAFF MEMBER AS A
CANDIDATE FOR OFFICE

At issue is whether a rule adopted by the international executive board violates the union constitution or the ethical practices codes of the union. The rule requires an international staff member who decides to run for an international office (in this case regional director) to take a leave of absence (without compensation) and be subject to reassignment in the event that the staff member is an unsuccessful candidate.

The United Automobile, Aerospace and Agricultural Implement Workers of America (UAW) requires that an international staff member who decides to run against an officer or regional director make his intentions known and request an uncompensated leave of absence at least ninety days prior to the convention at which the election is held. In addition, that staff member is subject to reassignment in the event he is an unsuccessful candidate.

Prior to November 28, 1985, regional director Warren Davis met with the Region 2 staff to discuss his upcoming bid for reelection. During that meeting, staff member Gary Brandt advised Davis he could not support him. On February 4, 1986, Brandt advised President Bieber that he intended to become a candidate for Region 2 director. On February 28, Dick Shoemaker, administrative assistant to President Bieber, advised Brandt that the international union policy required him to accept a leave of absence effective March 2, 1986. Brandt replied objecting to the involuntary leave; he pointed out his opponent had not been placed on leave; he had offered to contribute to the caucus and to discuss his opposition to Davis with President Bieber. Brandt argued that the decision to remove him from the payroll violated his constitutionally protected right to seek office.

Brandt filed an appeal on March 10, 1986, from the decision of the international executive board to place him on a leave of absence. At a hearing before a two-member appeals committee of the board, Brandt argued that the personal leave policy violates his constitutional right as a member to seek election for regional director without conditions or reprisals. He further argued that the only purpose of the rule is to retaliate against a staff member who seeks office against an incumbent. The appeals committee responded that "the rule safeguards an important benefit to international staff members, guaranteeing them adequate opportunity to campaign in their respective regions without the burden of their assignments." The international executive board held on October 3, 1986, that placing Brandt on personal leave did not violate the union constitution.

The UAW constitution provides (Article 14) that appointed international representatives may be removed by the International president subject to the approval of the international executive board.

Brandt appealed to the Public Review Board on October 16, 1986. This board is a private body of seven distinguished arbitrators and neutrals established in 1957 under the UAW constitution (Article 32). It is authorized on petition to review decisions of the national union's bodies and local union decisions to see that they conform to the union constitution, public law, and appropriate due process. A number of cases involve election issues.

Many Public Review Board cases involve members who claim their grievances against management were settled in violation of the union's duty of fair representation. The NLRB and the courts have virtually without exception sustained conclusions of the UAW Public Review Board in cases involving such grievances.

The decision of the Public Review Board in the Brandt case follows:

> We commence our discussion by noting that there is a well-settled line of demarcation between the rights of Union members as members and the rights of Union members as officers or agents. The right of a member in good standing to run for office in his or her Union may not be substantially abridged. On the other hand, the rights of appointed staff to run against those who appointed them while still maintaining their staff positions is subject to severe restriction. This is because it is recognized that in order to function effectively Union officers are entitled to a loyal staff devoted to carrying out their policies. Thus, while a member who holds a staff position may not be limited in his right to seek office in his Union and may not be retaliated against in terms of his membership rights for

doing so, this does not mean that the Union is restricted from affecting his job rights under those circumstances. Indeed, as pointed out by the International Union, the UAW's Constitution specifically provides that an International representative who seeks to run for local union office must first resign his staff position before doing so.

The Constitution, as Brandt correctly points out, contains no such requirement [applicable to an international representative who seeks to run for an international union office]. But the less onerous policy which appellant challenges here seems consistent with the philosophy of the Constitution. . . .

Brandt also complains that he has been retaliated against as a result of his unsuccessful effort to unseat Regional Director Davis. Again we believe that appellant Brandt has failed to carry his burden of proof. In the first place, the policy which was in effect when Brandt assumed his post as International Representative in October, 1973, provides specifically that unsuccessful challengers may be subject to reassignment and, while Brandt disclaims any knowledge of the policy prior to 1983, nevertheless he admits he was aware of it prior to his becoming a candidate in 1986. It is wholly comprehensible to us that in a political institution such as the UAW tensions might result from a lusty, vigorous political campaign waged between a Regional Director and one of his staff. Moreover, we can see how such tensions could interfere with the orderly workings of the Regional Director's staff which, as we previously observed, must operate effectively as a team in order to carry out the Director's and the Union's policies. It is true that appellant Brandt did withdraw as a candidate prior to the election and, moreover, pledged his support for Director Davis. But we would be naive in the extreme were we not to recognize that the withdrawal was in all probability motivated by the fact that Brandt came to the realization that his challenge was doomed to failure. While he may have felt that he could work effectively for Director Davis, the feeling may not have been shared by Mr. Davis himself. In any event, it was not Mr. Davis who effected the reassignment, but International President Bieber, who has the unquestioned authority to do this pursuant to both the Constitution and to the collective bargaining agreement, which governs the terms and conditions of employment of International representatives.

The decision of the International Executive Board is affirmed.[1]

A case reached the federal courts that involved a similar issue.[2] The court approved in *Tucker v. Bieber* the legitimacy of a union rule requiring appointed officers of the UAW who oppose an elected incumbent to declare their candidacy at least ninety days before the election and to take an unpaid leave of absence for that time. Tucker argued that the ninety-day rule is an illegal device developed by the union's controlling political party to stifle dissent. But the judge held that the Landrum-Griffin Act does not grant Tucker a legal right to hold a position on the union staff. His removal from appointed staff office did not cause him to lose membership rights or prohibit him from running for office, which he did and won on rerun.

Questions

1. Do you think public policy should establish a rule relating to how national unions should treat fully employed staff who choose to run for local or national union office? Or should such rules be left entirely to the political processes inside unions? What would be your judgment if the UAW rule imposed greater hardship on a staff member seeking elective office?

2. There are relatively few national unions that have adopted the idea of the Public Review Board. Do you think such boards are a good idea? Why have they not spread widely?

3. The UAW Public Review Board does on occasion overrule internal decisions of the UAW bodies, including the international executive board. What are the consequences of members, staff, and subordinate bodies having access to such a process? How can overuse be protected against?

4. How do you appraise the UAW rule affecting national union–appointed staff that seeks to run for local union office or national union office? What problems created this rule?

5. Would a similar rule, in your view, be appropriate for staff of local unions or other subordinate bodies?

6. What rules, if any, should apply in your view in public bodies that elect officers and have paid staff?

Notes

1. Public Review Board International Union, UAW, Case No. 787, August 29, 1987.
2. *Tucker v. Bieber,* DC E Mich, No. 86-4164 (January 19, 1989).

CASE 4

TRUSTEESHIP

The Labor-Management Reporting and Disclosure Act of 1959 provided for regulation by the Department of Labor and the courts of trusteeships or receiverships imposed by national unions on local unions or subordinate bodies. A trusteeship is defined by the statute to mean "any receivership, trusteeship, or other method of supervision or control whereby a labor organization suspends the autonomy otherwise available to a subordinate body under its constitution or bylaws" (sec. 3h). The purposes for which a trusteeship may be established are specified in section 302:

> Trusteeships shall be established and administered by a labor organization over a subordinate body only in accordance with the constitution and bylaws of the organization which has assumed trusteeship over the subordinate body and for the purpose of correcting corruption or financial malpractice, assuring the performance of collective bargaining agreements or other duties of a bargaining representative, restoring democratic procedures, or otherwise carrying out the legitimate objects of such labor organization.

The statute also provided that a trusteeship established by a labor organization

> in conformity with the procedural requirements of its constitution and bylaws and authorized or ratified after a fair hearing either before the executive board or before such other body as may be provided in accordance with its constitution or bylaws shall be presumed valid for a period of eighteen months from the date of its establishment and shall not be subject to attack during such period except upon clear and convincing proof that the trusteeship was not established or maintained in good faith for a purpose allowable under Section 302. After the expiration of eighteen months the trusteeship shall be presumed invalidated in any such proceeding and its discontinuance shall be decreed unless the labor organization shall show by clear and convincing proof that the continuance of the trusteeship is necessary for the purposes allowable under Section 302. (sec. 304)

The statute specifies reports that the labor organization imposing the trusteeship is required to file with the secretary of labor and specifies a fine of not more than $10,000 or imprisonment for more than one year, or both, for willful violation of the reports section of the law.

The same principles of regulation have been applied to unions composed of postal service employees and unions representing employees in most agencies of the executive branch of the federal government.

The 1959 statute led to the termination of a number of trusteeships, as in the provisional districts of the Mineworkers, so that initially terminations occurred more frequently than new trusteeships. National unions, moreover, revised their constitutions to comport with the new law and to make explicit the extent of authority provided to national unions in the statute.

The extent of trusteeship since 1959 is indicated in the following figures drawn from annual *Compliance Reports* of Labor-Management Services Administration, Department of Labor:

Fiscal Year	Initial Trusteeships	Terminated	Active June 30
1960	72	285	264
1965	145	135	226
1970	169	123	353
1975	223	200	636
1976	292	183	507
1980	109	212	540
1985	270	199	388
1986	256	222	449
1987	320	270	817

Between 1959 and 1987 the Department of labor was involved in 947 civil actions involving all provisions of the Landrum-Griffin statute, but only 8 of these cases were filed to enforce trusteeship provisions of the law.

Consider the following situation.

Lodge 837, International Association of Machinists (IAM), was opposed to the policies and dissatisfied with the services it received from District No. 9 of the IAM to which it was affiliated. Meetings of the local lodge became turbulent, and the advice of the international union, through a representative, was disregarded. An attorney was hired by the local against the orders of the international. The international then placed Lodge 837 under the "direction, control and supervision" of the District 9 secretary. He conducted regular meetings, approved expenditures, and the regular elections, which were won by the leaders of opposition to the international Union.

The international then suspended Lodge 837 and its officers and directed the trustee to take over the affairs of the local lodge. The suspended officers staged a sit-in, seized the union seal, advised the bank not to honor the signature of the trustee, and then urged the members to leave the IAM for an independent union. The suspended local officers were brought up on charges, found guilty, and expelled. Those expelled challenged the trusteeship in court.

Questions

1. International union representatives are often assigned to work out problems with and within local unions or other subordinate bodies. How should they approach such an assignment?

2. Does the bill of rights in the Landrum-Griffin law protect local officers who advocate that local members break away from the national organization? Is the advocacy of dual unionism protected under the law?

3. Has the enactment of the Landrum-Griffin law made national union officers more willing, or less willing, to take strong measures to impose policies adopted by the national union on recalcitrant local unions or subordinate bodies? Why? Do labor unions today impose too many or too few trusteeships?

4. May a trusteeship be imposed for the purpose of forcing a local union to affiliate with a district council and to raise dues as a result of the affiliation? May a trusteeship be imposed because a local is delinquent in paying a per capita tax increase it was challenging in court? May a trusteeship be imposed to prevent or terminate a wildcat strike? Is the purpose of a trusteeship always clear?

5. What constitutes "clear and convincing proof that the continuation of the trusteeship is necessary for a purpose allowable" under section 302 of the statute? Illustrate.

6. Compare a trusteeship instituted by an international union or a local union in accordance with the provisions of Title III of the Landrum-Griffin Act (1959) and a court-ordered trusteeship to eliminate corruption and racketeering instituted under the Organized Crime Control Act of 1970 (RICO). What are the objectives of the two types of trusteeships? What are their methods? How do they affect "the restoration of union democracy"?

6
Unions and Their Members

T he relationships of union members and their organizations encompass a wide range of activities and processes, and these interactions may vary significantly among individuals and from union to union. These relationships include admission standards, election procedures, union finances, union internal discipline and judicial systems, union press and communications arrangements, means to ascertain the views of members on policy issues, the responsiveness of union leadership to the often diverse interests of the members, issues of corruption of union officials, and some matters involved in collective bargaining, such as union security clauses or dues checkoff and other questions affecting the political and community activities of unions.

Many of these topics have been encompassed in the general discourse concerning union democracy. But a democratic union, however defined, is not necessarily well managed, financially well positioned, characterized by the best collective agreements under the circumstances, or free from corruption. Many issues of the relationship between a union and its members involve questions of the balance between the majority and the many minorities within the union.

By tradition, union constitution, and public law, union members are eligible to participate in the full range of union functions and activities, although not a large proportion generally do. Most citizens have many different interests that command their attention and commitment—family, social, cultural, religious, industrial, political, and economic interests and organizations—and the degree of involvement in the life of the union (at any one time) may vary significantly among members. As a result, the interest members take in the functioning of their unions varies greatly, and these variations also have an impact on the structure and functioning of the union. Thus, the administration of local unions differs, depending to some degree on the effects of the internal interests of the members. However, external factors can and do play an important role in union administration.

Work Environment

The industrial structure of the firms and establishments organized by a union undoubtedly has an important effect on the union's administration. Consider, for example, the problems of participation of members in unions in the airlines, some construction operations, over-the-road trucking, and migratory farm work compared to large industrial plants. The size, stability, and profitability of the firms in the industry also have their effects. The composition of the work force—age, sex, race, residence, educational level, and so forth—affects union governance. Typically the policies of employers largely determine such characteristics of the work force that has been assembled and hence many of the characteristics of union members. There may be significant differences among unions in the private sector, affected by the work force and workplaces of such industries as retailing, distribution, construction, utilities, and manufacturing. These differences in turn have some impact on the wage and benefit levels and rules of the different workplaces. The specific relationship between a union member and the local union, defined in terms of attitude, participation, and support, is thus affected by a range of external and internal factors.

Public Sector Environment

Unions in the public sector have characteristics that frequently vary significantly from those of unions in the private sector. Since membership of unions in the public sector has been growing rapidly, the importance of these unions has also grown. Among so-called public sector unions there are significant differences. The membership composition can be employees of federal, state, or local governments, and within these rubrics members can be professionals, white collar, blue collar, skilled, or unskilled. Although the structure and the administration of these unions have similarities to their counterparts in the private sector, the relationship of union members to their unions in the public sector is affected by additional factors not found in the private sector.

One feature is the widespread existence of civil service rules that affect the total employment situation of government employees, regardless of the provisions of a collective bargaining agreement. In many instances a union employee may exhaust the remedies provided in a collective bargaining agreement and then appeal the issue under civil service rules. The union expertise may be most helpful in this process.

Another feature of the public sector is the opportunity of unions and their members to affect directly the terms and conditions of employment through participation in the political arena. In the public sector the governmental determination of the terms and conditions of employment for its own employees is generally more extensive and the need to change these terms by legislation more frequent than the role of unions in the private sector. This is particularly evident in unions dealing in detailed collective bargaining directly with municipal governments, where the union members often are direct participants in the political process. This feature of public sector unions affects the relationship between union members and their unions.

One further aspect of the employment setting in the public sector affects the relationship between union members and their organizations. In most public employment the right to strike is withheld by statutes or by the courts. The attachment of members to their organizations and the bonds among members are not influenced by the picket line. The ballot alone may not develop the same intensity of the relationship.

Elections

Officers of national unions are elected by their delegates at national union conventions or by direct vote of the membership in a few unions. There has been considerable debate over the years as to the merits and demerits of each method, but each national union makes its own choice. National officers under either arrangement often run unopposed, so reelection is common. Nevertheless, the national officials are responsible and accountable to the membership, and opposition does arise and expresses itself in various ways when officials fail to take adequate cognizance of the needs or desires of the membership.

In local unions there is much more direct participation by members, and there is much more turnover of officials. The policies and actions of local officers have a more direct impact on the union members, and the interactions of officers and members and the rivalries among candidates are more immediate and personal. The participation of members in union elections is often a function of the members' satisfaction with the union's administration and with the union's attainment of the members' high priority goals.

Finances

The costs of running a union are financed by periodic dues and assessments paid by the members These dues are typically paid to the local by checkoff by the employer on a signed authorization of the employee (member) or by dues collection paid at the union office or to a union steward. The local typically makes per capita payments based on membership to the national union, as well as to some intermediate bodies. Local dues are generally set by a vote of the members, and when dues are to be raised, the issue frequently creates considerable attention. Membership participation in such a vote is ordinarily high.

Duty of Fair Representation

A union that has gained representation rights in a bargaining unit is required to represent all employees in the unit, regardless of whether they are members of the union. The union's duty to provide fair representation to all may be a difficult and costly proposition. The courts have interpreted this to mean that nonmembers of the union must be provided with equal access and opportunity to the union-management grievance procedure, including arbitration and litigation, which may be costly. The same standards of representation must be afforded to nonmembers as to the members, although in most situations the nonmembers are under no obligation to share in the costs of such union services. Thus, while the nonmember shares in all the benefits obtained by the union in the collective bargaining process, they may have no obligation to defray the costs.

In situations where the union has negotiated a collective bargaining agreement that includes a union shop provision, the nonmember is required either to join the union or to pay an agency shop fee to it. A union and an employer may agree that an agency service fee be deducted from each employee's pay check. However, where the checkoff of dues is not provided for in the contract, the nonmember is obliged to proffer the agency service fee. Failure to pay the fee can result in discharge, a penalty the courts accept as fair.

The question of how to define an appropriate agency service fee has also been raised in the courts. Nonmembers and their supporters have challenged the dues payment obligation imposed by a union shop agreement, contending nonmembers should not be required to contribute to any union costs except those incurred for collective bargaining and grievance administration activities. Courts have generally agreed that costs of union activities conceded by all to be political or ideological cannot be charged to nonmembers. But what of costs incurred in organizing nonmembers or in protecting the union's jurisdiction? The cost of running a union meeting may be considered legitimate, but what of the free coffee and beer offered at the meeting? If a politician is invited to speak, do these expenses have a different status? And what of the costs of social activities? There is also the cost of keeping accurate records and accounts in such a fashion so as to be able to set a service agency fee that accurately reflects collective bargaining and grievance administration activities.

Public Regulation

The Landrum-Griffin Act states that "in the public interest . . . it is essential that labor organizations, employers, and their officials adhere to the highest standards of responsibility and ethical conduct in administering the affairs of their organizations." Unions at all levels are required to hold elections at stipulated intervals. Members are guaranteed a reasonable opportunity to nominate candidates and run for office, and their right to criticize candidates and union policies is secured. Officers are prohibited from using union funds to promote the election of any candidate and are enjoined from disseminating propaganda for any candidate unless equivalent opportunities are given to the opposition. Union officials are required to file information relating to the financial affairs of the union, its constitutional provisions, the names and salaries of its officers, and financial dealings raising potential conflicts of interest. Further, the secretary of labor is empowered to investigate union elections and to bring suit to overturn any election whose outcome might be affected by a violation of law or a breach of the union's constitution and bylaws.

The administration of these detailed statutory provisions raises many questions of interpretation in drawing the lines of the limits of public regulation of union government and the relation of union members to their union organization and officers. These limits are under continuing review in the administrative processes of the Labor Department and in the courts.

Suggested Reading

Benjamim Aaron, Joyce M. Najita, and James L. Stern, eds., *Public-Sector Bargaining,* 2d ed., Industrial Relations Research Association Series (Washington, D. C.: Bureau of National Affairs, 1988).

Derek C. Bok and John T. Dunlop, *Labor and the American Community* (New York: Simon and Schuster, 1970).

Corruption and Racketeering in the New York City Construction Industry, Interim Report by the New York State Organized Crime Task Force (Ithaca, N. Y.: ILR Press, New York State School of Industrial Labor Relations, Cornell University, 1988).

Martin S. Estey, *The Unions: Structure, Development and Management,* 3d ed. (Harcourt Brace Jovanovich, 1981).

Richard B. Freeman and James L. Medoff, *What Do Unions Do?* (New York: Basic Books, 1984).

John Herling, *Right to Challenge: People and Power in the Steelworkers Union* (New York: Harper & Row, 1972).

Barry T. Hirsch and John T. Addison, *The Economic Analysis of Unions: New Approaches and Evidence* (Boston: Allen and Unwin, 1986).

Jerome M. Rosow, ed., *Teamwork: Joint Labor-Management Programs in America* (New York: Pergamon Press, 1986).

CASE 1
1977 UNITED STEELWORKERS OF
AMERICA ELECTION

On September 15, 1976, Chicago-Gary District director Edward Sadlowski, 38, officially announced his candidacy for the presidency of the then 1.4-million member United Steelworkers of America. Sadlowski, a dissident candidate, headed a slate for the five offices that would face Lloyd McBride, 60, St. Louis District director, the choice of retiring Steelworkers' President I.W. Abel and the head of the union's administration ticket. Abel had been unopposed in 1973, but the union's compulsory retirement rule at age 65 precluded his candidacy in the 1977 election. The Steelworkers elected its officers by direct referendum of the membership rather than by convention delegates,as do most other labor organizations.

Sadlowski came to prominence in 1974 when he defeated an Abel-backed candidate for the directorship of Chicago-Gary District 31, the largest in the Steelworkers' union. In that election, after Sadlowski had first lost narrowly, evidence of election abuses forced the union to declare a rerun, which Sadlowski won by a two-to-one margin. Sadlowski was inexperienced as a negotiator and administrator but was an articulate candidate.

In March 1973 the union and the basic steel industry coordinating committee had announced sixteen months in advance that they had adopted an experimental negotiating agreement (ENA) that would govern their negotiations following the expiration of their agreements in 1974. The ENA provided that there would be no strike or lockout at the expiration of the agreement and all national issues not resolved through collective bargaining would be submitted to a panel of arbitrators for final and binding decision. The ENA agreement would not extend to local issues. For the first time in the history of basic steel negotiations, local unions were given the right to strike over local issues with the approval of the international union president. This innovative agreement that was applied in the 1974 and 1977 negotiations was developed to avert crisis bargaining and to stabilize basic steel production and employment. It sought to eliminate the tendency on the part of customers to stockpile steel with overtime in anticipation of contract expiration and the possibility of a strike or lockout, and it reduced the subsequent layoff of steelworkers as inventories were reduced.[1]

Sadlowski had publicly criticized the ENA as a "secret deal" with employers that gave away the right to strike, and he was committed to end it. He argued that Abel and, implicitly, McBride ran the Steelworkers from the top down and had lost touch with the union rank and file. McBride generally supported Abel's policies, although he expressed an open mind regarding a continuation of ENA. This conflict over ENA attracted outside press attention.

Another reason for some press interest in the election was the alleged impact the outcome would have on the political orientation of the AFL-CIO. Liberal outsiders supported Sadlowski on the grounds that the AFL-CIO was on the threshold of major change. George Meany was 82, and it was said that his successor, at least initially, would not command the same degree of influence on the AFL-CIO executive council. Further, it was believed there had developed a steady polarization between the Meany loyalists: Abel and the leaders of the building trades and others and the liberal opposition that had formed the core of labor support for the McGovern ticket in 1972 when Meany remained neutral and refused to endorse the national Democratic party ticket. This split was also said to reflect difference on foreign policy and Vietnam.

In many respects, therefore, the election was as much a referendum on Abel as a contest between McBride and Sadlowski. McBride was the loyalist; he was supportive of ENA, politically moderate, and likely to carry on Abel's policies. Sadlowski was committed to "union democracy," direct membership ratification of basic steel union contracts, and the advocacy of income redistribution and liberal foreign policy positions.

By early 1976, Sadlowski had begun to explore in earnest the possibility of putting together a slate to replace Abel in 1977. With the support of Victor Reuther, the brother of former UAW president Walter Reuther, labor lawyer Joseph Rauh, and some assistance from Harvard professor John Kenneth Galbraith, Sadlowski began to build his circle of contacts within the union and among Democratic party liberals. He also sought and received commitments from a number of key workers in Arnold Miller's successful campaign to unseat longtime United Mine Workers' president W.A. "Tony" Boyle.

At the Las Vagas convention in August 1976, Abel opened the defense of his administration's record and launched the first of many attacks on Sadlowski. At a press conference on August 29, Abel emphasized the convention's support of the ENA. In a reference to Sadlowski's outside supporters, Abel said that he was "gravely concerned about outsiders trying to undermine the United Steelworkers." Without mentioning any names, he said of them,

They insist on belittling your progress and distorting your record. This attack is unmatched in its harshness and intensity. They would like the influence and prestige this union has built up with 40 years of struggle and hard work. Some of them would like to become your advisors, consultants, or even kingmakers. Others would like to parade behind our reputation as a sound effective union and bend our union to their narrow selfish purposes. Some like your political power and would like to use it to pursue their own little adventures. In short, they want to take over.

No dissident groups are going to shape the policies of this union. No news media representatives will have a vote here. No amount of outside coaching or meddling is going to capture this convention. You may have my word on it. And that goes for RAFT, SURF, the National Conference of Steelworkers, the Steelworkers Fight Back Committee, the so-called U.S. Labor Party, the Socialist Labor Party, the so-called Progressives, the Communist Party, the Fascist Party, the Nazis, the Trotskyites, the Maoists, the Republicans, Socialists, Democrats, Conservatives, America Firsters or whatever.

Sadlowski chose to lay low at the convention, apparently recognizing that he had few supporters among delegates and staff representatives. He addressed the convention only a few times from the floor and was drowned out by boos when he spoke out against a proposal to strengthen union rules prohibiting officers from involvement in the Ku Klux Klan, the Communist party, and other "extremist" organizations. Sadlowski charged that the proposal was an antidemocratic smear tactic against him as he had continuously been accused of being a Communist during the convention.

Issues

The issues raised during the campaign can be separated into two groups: (1) those concerning the internal management of the union and its collective bargaining role and (2) those concerning the election process.

Most of the union issues were raised by Sadlowski as the challenger. His most prominent issue position was his opposition to the ENA and what he termed "secretive centralized negotiation." In calling for greater "union democracy," direct membership ratification of union contracts, and an end to the no-strike clause of the ENA, Sadlowski charged that the USW leadership had lost touch with the rank and file. Under Abel's leadership, according to Sadlowski, "there has been too much talk and concern about productivity and nothing about the problems of the average workers. The only time a company acquiesces is when we hit the bricks or threaten to do it, and they never talk about that." Abel's earlier appearance in full-page newspaper advertisements and posters paid for by U.S. Steel calling for increased productivity was used to support Sadlowski's claims.

Other issues that enabled Sadlowski to play upon "a growing gap between elected union officials and the rank and file" included increases in dues and officers' salaries. In 1974, a constitutional convention had increased dues and raised international officers' annual salaries to $75,000. Sadlowski was committed to cut union salaries, reduce dues, and deal with long-standing rank-and-file objections to the size of the union staff.

Beyond commitments to "bring the leadership back into the Steelworkers union," Sadlowski also carried a message of what he termed "progressive union democracy" to both union halls and outside liberal supporters: "We're not only attempting to take on the hierarchy of the Steelworkers union because of the problems that exist on the shop floor. The ultimate goal is to make this union into the most aggressive and progressive institution this country has ever seen. We're capable of taking this institution into the streets and solving major problems that confront each and every one of us as American citizens or as citizens of the world." Further, Sadlowski opposed many of the AFL-CIO's foreign policy positions, including labor's earlier support of the Vietnam War: "The direction of the George Meanys and the J. Lovestones have to change. McBride is more conservative than H.L. Hunt."

But while Sadlowski was making the most of union problems and the political orientation of organized labor, Abel and McBride were turning Sadlowski's outside support and his lack of negotiating experience into an issue in the campaign. McBride charged that Sadlowski was the tool of left-leaning "outsiders" and "limousine liberals," principally Rauh, Reuther, and Galbraith: "I'm really convinced that the brain behind Sadlowski is Rauh. This is a union of Steelworkers. This is not a union to be manipulated by anyone outside of the union structure."

Abel and McBride argued that direct referendum ratification pointed up Sadlowski's lack of knowledge and interest in bargaining and the true business of the union: "We then run the risk of having some area ratify the contract while our members working for another company reject it. We would then be on strike against part of the industry and have a contract with another part of the industry, and thereby would destroy our ability to bargain industry-wide." Sadlowski claimed that this problem could be easily avoided by requiring a single vote on ratification in each of the major sectors, and he accused McBride of twisting the issue, but he never presented substantive proposals to adapt the negotiation process to direct ratification.

Reaction among informed commentators and industry spokesmen to the negotiation issues raised in the campaign was uniformly negative. A.H. Raskin, *New York Times* labor reporter, termed the election a dramatic contest between the traditional "business union" leaders and the "ideologues" but felt that the issues were not being drawn properly. Bruce Johnston, chief negotiator for the steel companies, chided both candidates for conducting personality campaigns and failing to discuss the ENA in any reasonable manner.

Sadlowski's response to steel industry criticism was as follows: "It is clear that the steel industry is worried that out slate is going to win and that we will have a strong and democratic union again which looks out for the membership first. Johnson and the steel industry know that if we get in, our business will be handled differently; we will put an end to secret under-the-table negotiations and submit all contracts to members for ratification." The two major election process issues were Sadlowski's contributions from outside sources and the use of the union's internal machinery to generate funds, publicity, and votes for McBride.

Sadlowski's outside supporters frankly admitted that they were concerned less with his role as an administrator than with his potential as a spokesman for liberal causes on the AFL-CIO executive board. As one fund-raising appeal from John Kenneth Galbraith put it:

> Sadlowski is in the forefront of a movement that is sweeping the Steelworkers and many other unions—a movement to turn the American labor movement around and make it into the democratic progressive political and economic force its founders intended it to be.
>
> Sadlowski and the movement he leads believe that the Vietnam War could not have continued if America's labor leadership had stood against it. He would like to place the union in the forefront of pollution control, and the health and safety of American working people. He doesn't buy the cliché that more defense spending makes more jobs regardless of the consequences. He thinks that labor should be seriously committed to decent health care and rights of minorities and women. And, perhaps most important, Sadlowski is fighting to bring democracy to labor and to end efforts to intimidate or frighten those who speak out for their rights.

In addition to contributions from Rauh, Reuther, and Galbraith, Sadlowski apparently received support from a number of unions. He argued that his outside support, both union and from other sources, was legitimate because organized labor would always have a major impact on public issues, and it was always appropriate to seek to bring a greater degree of democracy to institutions.

A major argument for outside assistance, however, is the influence of the established union hierarchy in all union elections. McBride inherited the support of almost all of the Abel "official family," including the 850 paid field staff representatives, the executive board, and a large majority of local union officials. All staff members, including those in Sadlowski's Chicago-Gary district, were hired directly by the international union. Almost all contributed to the McBride campaign. In addition, Sadlowski charged that staff ran the McBride campaign on union time, used the Steelworkers' newspaper, *Steel Labor,* to build up the Abel administration and McBride's own record, and they were under great pressure to deliver their districts.

This last accusation formed the base of a significant part of Sadlowski's campaign, including, some said, a long-term strategy to overturn the first election and win a rerun. By questioning the fairness of Abel's control over the election machinery and asking for a greater role for the U.S. Department of Labor in conducting the election, Sadlowski kept the issue alive. Every international Steelworkers' election after 1959 had been marred by charges of fraud. The background to Sadlowski's own rerun election in 1974 made this an especially potent issue.

Sadlowski and his campaign organizers were publicly worried about abuses on two levels: first, the withholding of information such as the location of polling places and the up-to-date list of registered members, and second, the counting and tallying of votes, particularly at the local level. Without knowing the location of the union's 6,000 polling places in advance, Sadlowski representatives would not be able to place observers to monitor ballot counting. Sadlowski would be able to place observers at district offices where the returns from the locals were tallied, but the potential for abuse was most serious at small locals where staff representatives and local officials did most of the election work.

Campaign Developments

In late November 1976, Abel asked Secretary of Labor William J. Usery for "technical assistance" in conducting the election. Abel asked Usery to "immediately assume the responsibility for answering all written inquiries" on a nonbinding basis.

Two days later, Sadlowski sent a telegram to Usery requesting full Department of Labor supervision of the election. Labor Department spokesmen said that the agency would not make a decision on the request until it had consulted with the candidates, but they emphasized that the Landrum-Griffin Act did not give the department preelection enforcement powers. Other sources pointed out that the department had only 500 employees to cover 6,000 polling places and argued that Sadlowski was actually "laying the ground for a post-election challenge."

McBride, when advised of Sadlowski's telegram, issued a statement to the effect that he did not oppose Labor Department supervision but felt the decision should be made by the union officers, and not himself or Sadlowski. He added, "Mr. Sadlowski seems to have forgotten that we have close to 200,000 members in Canada. I do not believe that they recognize the jurisdiction of the U.S. Department of Labor in their country, nor should they."

Also in November, Sadlowski brought two suits in the U.S. District Court of Pittsburgh. One was to obtain information concerning the location of polling places and the procedures for placing observers to monitor the count. The second was a preliminary injunction banning what he felt to be bias against him in *Steel Labor*. He also requested access to the membership through a free mailing or space in the newspaper to offset past bias. On November 24, the second suit was settled out of court. The three-part settlement was as follows:

1. All three parties—Sadlowski, McBride, and the union—would have the right to screen in advance the election material appearing in *Steel Labor*. Unresolved differences would be settled by the court.

2. The union was to pay for a one-time joint mailing of both candidates' literature to all voting members. This literature was to be submitted to both of the other parties for criticism and could not contain personal attacks on anyone but the opposing candidate.

3. The losing candidate would not be able to challenge the election on the basis of coverage in *Steel Labor* in violation of the Landrum-Griffin Act.

On December 1, 1976, Secretary of Labor Usery rejected Sadlowski's request that the department supervise the election: "The suggestion that this Department supervise the upcoming election of International Officers of the USW is not practical in view of our limited manpower resources." Sadlowski immediately responded to the effect that Usery's refusal put the department in league with the Abel administration and was "a blow to trade union democracy and to full and fair enforcement of the Landrum-Griffin Act." By late December, both Abel and AFL-CIO president Meany had publicly endorsed McBride. Meany's action was unprecedented and was accompanied by the following statement: "It is deeply disturbing that democratic unions . . . once again face an effort to control their policies and programs by monied interests outside the union."

In early January, the Department of Labor announced a four-part program of assistance in the conduct of the election. First, the department would provide nonbinding "technical assistance" concerning issues raised in writing by the candidates. Second, it would observe the union's special training sessions for tellers. Third, it would send two compliance officers to each of the union's twenty-five districts. Finally, department representatives would tally the results received from the 6,000 local polling places.

On January 31, the candidates met in a half-hour question-and-answer session on NBC's "*Meet the Press*." Neither candidate raised any new issues. Sadlowski criticized the extent to which the union leadership had become "compatible with industry rather than compatible with the membership" and declared his opposition to the ENA because it had contributed to the union's inability to keep "abreast of the profit structure of the steel industry." McBride held primarily to the issue of outside contributors and sought to tie Sadlowski to employers and business executives of "giant corporations."

Election Aftermath

McBride and his slate won the election with 57 percent of the 578,000 votes cast. Although Sadlowski had done well in the large basic steel locals, Mc-Bride overwhelmed him by scoring heavily in small locals, Canada, and the nonbasic steel sectors.

In 1978 the Steelworkers amended its constitution to include the follow-ing paragraph: "No candidate (including a prospective candidate) for any position set forth in Article IV, Section 1, and supporters of a candidate may solicit or accept financial support, or any other direct or indirect support of any kind (except an individual's own volunteered personal time) from any non-member." The offices referred to include president, secretary, treasurer, two vice-presidents, twenty-five district directors, and national director for Canada.

Sadlowski challenged the new amendment to the union constitution. In 1982 the Supreme Court by a five-to-four vote decided that the provision did not violate the Labor-Management Reporting and Disclosure Act (1959) giv-ing every union member the right to assemble freely with other members and to express at union meetings their views about candidates in union elections or any business properly before the meeting. Nor, in the majority opinion of the Court, did the provision limit the rights of members to initiate an action in the courts or before government agencies as would be prohibited by the Bill of Rights, sec. 101(a)(4), of the 1959 statute.[2]

Questions

1. It has been said that a labor organization tends to have a one-party sys-tem of governance, that is, the administration. What is the role of elec-tions in these circumstances?

2. From the death of Philip Murray, the first president of the Steelworkers, in 1952 through the Sadlowski-McBride contest in 1977, there were a number of contested elections in this national union. Indeed in 1965 I.W. Abel unseated David McDonald who had followed Murray as president in 1953. What are the consequences of frequent contested elections in a national union? Do labor organizations develop continuing "political parties" with continuing electoral conflict? Would that be desirable?

3. How should contests of office in labor unions be financed? Do you think other unions or employers should be free to provide financial support to a candidate for union office? Should the relatives or family of the can-didate be allowed to provide such support?

4. Would not a simple rule providing for the disclosure of all contributions be adequate?

5. Is the Labor Management Reporting and Disclosure Act (1959) an adequate standard for the public interest in internal union affairs? What, if any, changes would you make?

6. Unions often claim to be democratic organizations. What tests would you apply? To what other organizations would you compare them?

7. Why are there more changes in officers in local unions as a consequence of periodic elections than in the elections of national union officers?

Notes

1. For a discussion of collective bargaining in the steel industry see Jack Stieber, "Steel," in *Collective Bargaining: Contemporary American Experience,* ed. Gerald G. Somers, Industrial Relations Research Association Series (Madison, Wis.: Industrial Relations Research Association, 1980), pp. 151–208.

2. *United Steelworkers of America v. Sadlowski,* 102 S. Ct. 2339 (1982).

CASE 2
REFUSAL TO PAY AGENCY SHOP FEE

The case involves an agency shop clause included in the collective bargaining agreement between the Detroit Board of Education and the Detroit Federation of Teachers, an affiliate of the American Federation of Teachers. The clause specifies that teachers who fail to pay the agency fee are subject to discharge. The court considered the case in the context of a teacher who had been with the Detroit school system for many years.

Anne B. Parks initially paid the fee under protest. Later, however, she refused to make further payments, and the school board discharged her at the union's request. After appealing to the State Tenure Commission, Parks was reinstated on the grounds that the procedures under the tenure act were not followed. The Wayne County Circuit Court reversed the commission's decision, and a state appeals court subsequently upheld the circuit court.

Reviewing the Michigan Public Employment Relations Act (PERA) provisions concerning payment of agency fees as a condition of employment, the Michigan Supreme Court observes that it has been guided by federal court decisions construing similar provisions of the National Labor Relations Act. The court says:

We find it inconceivable that, in adopting the phrase "to require as a condition of employment" from federal law, the Michigan Legislature did not also intend to adopt the construction placed on that language by the federal courts. Even without this authority, we would find it difficult to allow any other interpretation than the obvious—"condition of employment" as used in [PERA] means that employment may be conditioned on payment of the agency service fees.

The court finds that although discharge is not always a remedy for the violation of a condition of employment, "it is also clear that discharge can be a remedy, if so provided in the contract, as it was in this case." The court says the argument that remedies less severe than discharge preclude dismissal as a permissible remedy "misses the point," adding: "Of course, nothing forbids the union and employer from agreeing on a less harsh remedy. A union and an employer could agree the agency service fees would be automatically deducted from each employee's pay check. . . . The collective bargaining agreement here, however, does not require or expressly permit agency service fee deductions in the absence of a signed authorization by the employee."

The court notes that it has consistently construed the PERA as the dominant law regulating public labor relations and that the PERA prevails when there is a conflict between it and another statute. According to the court, the express language in the PERA provides sufficient grounds to find inapplicable in this case the "reasonable and just cause" for discharge provision in the teacher tenure act.

The court adds that although the "reasonable and just cause" standard of the tenure act has been construed to forbid discharge unless the action "bears a rational and specific relationship to a detrimental effect on the school and the students," the tenure law was not designed to cover labor disputes. The court states:

The procedures of the teacher tenure act are designed to protect a tenured teacher from discharge for improper reasons, reasons other than those of professional competency. Of necessity, the often subjective determination of a teacher's competency must be carefully scrutinized. The teacher tenure act provides that prior to discharge a tenured teacher is entitled to written notice of the reasons for discharge at least 60 days prior to the end of the school year. A formal hearing must be held before the controlling board within 45 days. . . . An appeal by right to the State Tenure Commission is provided. . . . We cannot conclude that the Legislature intended to also use this elaborate procedure for the simple purpose of determining whether a teacher has, in fact, paid his agency service fees.

The court says that a teacher contesting the claim that the agency fees were not paid, or contesting the legality of the fee, "is free to file an unfair labor practice complaint" under the PERA. According to the court, "the procedure set forth in PERA for the adjudication of unfair labor practices before the MERC [Michigan Employment Relations Commission] is more than sufficient to satisfy any due process concerns that appellants may have."[1]

Questions

1. What is the purpose of an agency fee? How does it differ from union dues?

2. What are various ways in which a collective bargaining agreement might deal with individuals in the bargaining unit who decide not to pay an agency fee?

3. State the case for and the case against discharge from employment as a method to deal with nonpayment of an agency fee. In a setting in which the union seeks to attract members, is a request for discharge an effective instrument to build the union?

4. In the education field, what is the case for tenure? What precisely does tenure mean? What is the relation between tenure and collective bargaining?

5. More generally, are collective bargaining and civil service rules consistent? Which should govern when there is conflict?

Note

1. The source for this case is *Detroit Board of Education and Detroit Federation of Teachers v. Anne B. Parks, et al.,* Mich. Sup. Ct., cases 65818, 65819, 65820, 65821, filed June 27, 1983 as reported in Bureau of National Affairs, *Government Employee Relations Report,* October 10, 1983, pp. 2013–2014.

CASE 3
SERVICES TO NONMEMBERS

The National Treasury Employees Union (NTEU) represents about 120,000 federal employees, of whom about 65,000 are dues-paying union members. The NTEU advised bargaining unit employees that it would be union policy to provide attorney representation for grievances and other matters only to union members. Under the policy, nonmembers were to be limited to representation by shop stewards. The U.S. Customs Service and the Nuclear Regulatory Commission filed an unfair labor practice charge against the union, and the Federal Labor Relations Authority (FLRA) subsequently ordered the NTEU to cease its policy.

The U.S. court of appeals agreed with the FLRA conclusion that the union breached its duty of fair representation. Writing for the court, Judge Harry T. Edwards said the "plain language" of the law "requires the Union to represent all bargaining unit employees 'without discrimination and without regard to labor organization membership' and means exactly what it says."

Judge Edwards rejects the union's arguments that "adequate representation" is furnished to nonmembers by chapter officials or shop stewards and that the attorney service for union members is merely an internal benefit, which need not be extended to nonmembers. Judge Edwards calls the NTEU arguments "patently meritless." The court says:

> The principle underlying the duty of fair representation in the private sector is that "the exclusive agent's statutory authority to represent all members of a designated unit includes a statutory obligation to serve the interests of all members without hostility or *discrimination* toward any, to exercise its discretion with complete good faith and honesty, and to avoid arbitrary conduct." . . . The duty of fair representation does not establish an objective standard of "adequate representation" that the union must meet as a minimum, and that, once met, the union may use as a basis upon which to discriminate between members and nonmembers. Rather, under the duty of fair representation, a union may adopt virtually *any* non-arbitrary standard for providing representation of individual employees, so long as the standard adopted is applied in a nondiscriminatory manner with respect to all unit employees, i.e., members and nonmembers alike.

The court says in this case, "representation by attorneys, who are formally trained and certified in practice of law, is demonstrably different from representation by chapter officers and stewards." Furthermore, the court notes, the attorney representation "pertains directly to enforcement of the fruits of collective bargaining," so the union may not provide such a benefit exclusively for union members.[1]

Questions

1. How did the doctrine of the duty of fair representation develop in the courts? (This is the duty of a union to represent all employees in the

bargaining unit without hostile discrimination and without regard to labor organization membership.)

2. Does the duty of fair representation require a union to take every grievance to arbitration? every discharge case? What distinctions are permissible?

3. If the union must treat all employees—members and nonmembers—without distinction, why should a nonmember join the union? Can there be no rewards for union membership?

4. In the federal government, the scope of collective bargaining is very narrow compared to the private sector or to other levels of government. Does this affect the capacity of unions to recruit members?

Note

1. The source for this case is National Treasury Employees Union v. Federal Labor Relations Authority, CA DC No. 83–1054, November 22, 1983, as reported in Bureau of National Affairs, *Daily Labor Report,* December 5, 1983, pp. A1–A2.

CASE 4
THE INDIVIDUAL EMPLOYEE AND THE RESPONSIBILITIES TO THE UNION

One of the most controversial cases decided by the British Columbia Labour Board involved a dispute not between a union and an employer but rather between a union and an employee. A potential conflict of interest between union and employee lurks in the background of the basic framework of collective bargaining. In recent years that theme in labor law—the rights of the individual in relation to those of the tradeunion—has surged to the forefront. Sometimes the employer sides with the employee, sometimes with the union, and sometimes it just wants to avoid the fallout from either side. The *Tottle* case put the issues rather starkly.

The Office and Technical Employees Union is the certified bargaining agent for some 3,500 office and technical employees of the B.C. Hydro. The collective bargaining relationship had existed for years, and in the spring the parties were negotiating for renewal of their agreement. They had considerable difficulty in arriving at a settlement that year for a variety of reasons, among them the difficulty of interpreting the precise wage stabilization guidelines for that unit in the light of its peculiar history and the independent effort of the new provincial government to impose considerable wage restraint on public servants, including employees of public utilities.

The union conducted meetings throughout the province in May to advise its members of these problems at the bargaining table and to take a strike vote. The executive explained to the members that before it called a total strike, it would try out a variety of partial guerrilla actions: an overtime ban, work-to-rule, and then rotating strikes. The union received an 88 percent strike mandate from its members.

In June the union strike committee met to plan the precise timetable for its selective job action: first the overtime ban, then the work-to-rule campaign, and then the partial strike. The last was quite a shrewd scheme. Employees in certain crucial departments of Hydro (for example, those who sent out the bills and processed the checks) would be pulled off their jobs. Those in the "nonproductive areas" (presumably the union meant by this those less immediately productive) would be left at work and drawing their salary. Overall the union would be able to put maximum pressure on Hydro at the least net loss to the overall unit.

Left by itself there was a major flaw in that plan: it involved a very uneven distribution of sacrifice among the members of the unit. Some employees would be pulled off work completely, receiving no earnings from the Hydro and just minimal strike pay from the union. Others would remain at work drawing their full pay. So the union committee hit on the idea of a special fund as part of the job action program. Those members not going on strike would each contribute 10 percent of their earnings, leaving them with 90 percent of their normal pay for this period. In turn, that would enable the union to pay those key members who were pulled off their jobs up to 70 percent of their normal earnings (that differential being justified by the fact that the strikers were not actually having to work during that period).

The union considered this to be an equitable plan to equalize the relative burdens of its job action strategy, but it did not feel that it should compel members to participate if they chose not to do so. The union was loathe to force its members to pay any proportion of their regular earnings, although many trade unions do make these special assessments of working members during a strike. But the union executive did have the right to direct its members to go on strike (once it had obtained the majority strike vote). So the bulletin to the membership gave them a choice: either participate in the special job action, whether by coming off the job as directed or paying into the fund to finance the selective strikes, or simply go on full strike. A very few members (about twenty) took the latter option. The vast majority participated in the job action plan. A handful, the most prominent being Tottle, refused to do either. Tottle did join in the overtime ban and the work-to-rule, neither of which made any tangible difference in his workday. But when the partial strikes were called, Tottle refused either to play his stated role (which was to stay on the job and contribute the equivalent of one day's pay every two weeks, for total of four days' pay) or to go out on full strike himself.

Eventually, by the end of the summer, the union tactics secured an acceptable contract settlement from the Hydro. The degree of movement that occurred as a result of the job action plan can be appreciated from the union's calculation regarding Tottle's personal situation. The difference between the Hydro's last offer before the partial strike began and the final offer accepted by the union amounted to $1,800 for Tottle in the two-year collective agreement. For that reason the union believed that it could not leave Tottle (and the other dissidents) unscathed.

Notices were served on Tottle et al. of disciplinary proceedings, which were then conducted meticulously under the union's constitution. First there was a hearing before the union's executive board, at which Tottle was found guilty of working during the strike for thirty-nine days (that is, for failing to have obeyed the legal strike directive as the option given him for nonparticipation in the job action plan). The executive board ordered that Tottle pay a fine of $25 a day for every day so worked (totaling $975) plus accept a further suspension of thirty days from the union (which meant that he would have to be absent from work at the Hydro for that period). But these executive board rulings were only recommendations. They still had to be approved or rejected by the local membership at its regular meetings. In fact the rulings were approved by the membership by a 90 percent margin, and Tottle and the other members charged were told that their discipline was now in effect.

Several of the dissidents now decided to comply—paying the fines and accepting the suspensions. Others, especially Tottle, continued to ignore the entire process: the executive board hearing, the membership meetings, and the opportunity to appeal under the international constitution, and then the dunning letter from the union for payment of the fine. The union proceeded to go through the entire procedure once more, this time to impose internal union discipline for refusal to comply with the earlier discipline. The process of notice of the charges, executive board hearing, membership confirmation, and notice to Tottle of his right to appeal was followed to the letter. This time the penalty was more serious: expulsion from the union.

That last was a sanction that Tottle could not blandly ignore. Why? Because the union had a contract with the Hydro requiring that employees covered by the agreement "as a condition of continued employment at the Hydro become and remain members in good standing with the Union." The price of Tottle's imbroglio with the union would be his job with the Hydro. When the union demanded that Hydro fire Tottle after his expulsion, Hydro brought the entire matter to the Labour Board. After considering a variety of legal arguments under the Labour Code and the collective agreement, the board concluded that the union's legal position was well founded and that the Hydro was obligated to dismiss Tottle. Feeling sure that Tottle was not that interested in becoming a martyr to the cause of union dissidence, a stay was put on that order for a period of time during which Tottle could reinstate himself in the union's good graces by complying with the original discipline. Tottle did pay the fine and accept the suspension, the union happily received him back in membership, and the Hydro was able to keep what it considered a "valued employee."

That merely avoided an unhappy ending to the Tottle tale. By no means did it detract from the significance of the board's general ruling about the kind of legal compulsion a trade union may exert over an individual employee. The facts of the *Tottle* case vividly illustrate the points that both sides are making in the polarized debate about the right-to-work movement. From the trade union perspective, this seemed a particularly appealing case from which to advocate its cause. The job action program was lawful. It was a restrained kind of strike action against the giant utility. It had been approved by a vast majority of the membership. And it turned out to be successful for everyone in obtaining a generous improvement in the employer's contract offer. Moreover, while Tottle stonewalled at every stage of the proceedings, the union meticulously observed all of the elements of due process: notice of charges, a full hearing, and extensive rights of appeal. Nor was this the action of a union bureaucracy out of touch with its members. The executive ruling had to be approved by membership vote, and it was approved overwhelmingly.

Questions

1. Should a union have the right to compel a dissident member to comply with its decisions about bargaining tactics? In effect the union "conscripted" Tottle to participate in that job action against his employer and purported to "tax away" part of his personal earnings for the general cause.

2. Should the union have the power to fine its members, to suspend employees from work for a period in order to enforce its own policies, and then further to enforce those measures by depriving Tottle of his "right to work" for the Hydro, which considered him to be a good employee?

3. The union scrupulously followed the procedures of its constitution and received support at every turn from the membership. Does this make any difference to your views on the previous questions?

4. What discipline should a labor organization be authorized to impose on its members?

Note

1. The sources for this case are Paul Weiler, *Reconcilable Differences, New Directions in Canadian Labour Law,* (Toronto: Carswell, 1980), pp. 121–24; *British Columbia Hydro and Power Authority and Office and Technical Employees Union, Local 378 and Christopher R. Tottle,* British Columbia, March 7, 1978, Decision No. 9/78.

Part III
Labor Unions and the Society

7
Labor and the Community

I n their classic analysis of trade unions in Great Britain, *Industrial Democracy*, Sidney Webb and Beatrice Webb reported that unions from their beginnings sought to achieve their objective of elevating the social position of their members by "three distinct instruments or levers": the method of collective bargaining, the method of legal enactment, and the method of mutual insurance.[1]

The method of collective bargaining, in the American experience, involves periodic negotiations with representatives of management over the terms and conditions of employment and the day-to-day administration of such agreements with resort to a grievance procedure and arbitration. The method of legal enactment includes in the United States the effort to secure supportive administrative rulings from executive departments and agencies at all levels of government or through judicial interpretation or supportive legislative enactment. The growth of labor organizations among public employees has increased resort to the method of legal enactment for employees in that work setting.

In Great Britain, as in the United States, mutual insurance historically referred to the provision of benefits from regular contributions by union members for some protection in the event of casualties such as death, accident, illness, or retirement or in the event of unemployment. These friendly society features of early labor organizations were vital in an era of fear among workers and their families of burial in potter's field, leaving a family without any financial resources, high accident rates in dangerous employment where life insurance could not be purchased or was prohibitive, and at a time when public programs of workers' compensation and social security were unknown. These friendly society benefits were significant to the development of many national unions in the United States, such as the Printers, Locomotive Engineers, Ironworkers, and Electricians, although beneficiary features developed more slowly than in the unions of England and Germany.[2] These benefits were adopted in part because it was believed that they tended to help keep members attached to the union during periods of unemployment.

In the past generation, the methods of collective bargaining and legal enactment in the United States have largely encompassed and replaced the functions performed by mutual insurance in an earlier era (save in the case of a few unions) with the growth of negotiated health and welfare and pension plans and with social legislation such as workers' compensation, unemployment insurance, social security, and a wide variety of other programs. Moreover, collective bargaining has supported and extended public programs such as supplemental unemployment benefits, the enforcement of legislative and administrative health and safety standards at the workplace, and safety committees.

Since the 1930s, with the transformation of the method of social insurance, American labor organizations appear also to have developed a new function with a wider constituency than their membership. It might be called the method of voluntary service to the local community and encompasses such activities as participation in the United Way and the Red Cross, some housing programs, education and training programs, and health care coalitions. Although some union members may be benefited, the focus of such activities is the larger community. The activities rely on voluntarism and joint consultation rather than on legislative enactment or negotiations in collective bargaining.

The method of voluntary community service is to be sharply distinguished from the policies adopted by a relatively few large local unions that have developed extensive welfare programs for their members financed by employer contributions negotiated under collective bargaining agreements.[3] These "welfare-state" local unions, such as Local 3 of the International Brotherhood of Electrical Workers in New York City and Local 688 of the Teamsters in St. Louis, established programs for such items as general and occupational education, retirement activities, credit plans, counseling, vacation facilities, travel tours, arts festivals, and housing and cooperative apartments. Such programs necessarily involve some diversion of resources, including scarce leadership talent that might otherwise be devoted to increasing wages and conventional benefits or other programs, but the membership of these "welfare-state" locals appears to support these activities rather than to insist on putting the money in the pay envelope. The "welfare-state" pattern in these cases seems to be the collective preference.

Unlike "welfare-state" activities, voluntary community service is intended primarily to benefit nonmembers and is not ordinarily paid for by employers pursuant to a collective bargaining agreement. The question may appropriately be asked as to why labor organizations are engaged, probably on an increasing scale, in such voluntary community service. There are a number of considerations at work, as reflected in a resolution adopted by an early AFL-CIO convention and by an executive council resolution more recently:

- The collective agreement does not meet the emergency needs of union members and their families for food, shelter, clothing and medical care caused by natural and man-made disasters such as hurricanes, floods, earthquakes, layoffs, strikes and riots.

- It is the responsibility of the union, therefore, to extend its services to its members and their families beyond the plant gates and the collective bargaining agreement with the neighborhood and the community as a whole by establishing effective organizational relationships with community agencies. . . .

- Such active labor participation in community affairs, on the policy making boards of agencies in developing needed new services, in social action for more and better facilities and in the application of collective bargaining techniques to consumer-merchant, patient-physician and tenant-landlord relationships, will help make communities more representative of the people and responsive to the people's needs.

- A by-product of labor's public service and concern for a better community for all is effective community and public relations for the trade union movement as a whole.[4]

All community service agencies in the private sector are called upon "to respect the rights of their employees to join unions within the spirit of the public policy of these United States." Moreover, agencies were called upon "to buy union-made goods and services as a normal part of their operating procedures."[5]

Such statements are a mixture of humanitarianism and self-interest, but that should be no criticism. Indeed, similar community-oriented policies have come to be widely adopted by many profit-making business enterprises. The Harvard George S. Dively Award for Corporate Public Initiative states:

> Business leaders across the country are becoming more actively involved with their public counterparts in collaborative efforts designed to help solve important social problems in such areas as education, job training, child care, delivery of health care services, economic development, the care of senior citizens, and community planning.
>
> To focus attention on these efforts and to encourage greater participation by other business leaders, the award is presented to a chief executive officer whose company is innovative in its approach to problem-solving and has made an outstanding contribution to the solution of important social needs.[6]

In responding to the 1986 award John T. Akers, president and chief executive officer of IBM, stated:

The educational imperative means a hundred IMBers in full-salary leave this year to teach and do administration in colleges and high schools with high enrollments of disadvantaged and disabled students' and a $20 million computer literacy program for high school students in 27 states.

Along with this major thrust a company like ours has a particular responsibility to insist on the need for balance between the sciences and humanities, including great works of art in sculpture or drama or music or painting.[7]

In responding for General Mills in 1987, A.B. Atwater, Jr., chairman and chief executive officer, reported:

We began with a revision of the set of objectives which each executive submits at the start of the fiscal year. These objectives are the bench mark to measure accomplishment for cash incentive purposes. We had historically asked for specific objectives in three broad areas: current financial performances; long-term strategy and manpower development. We now include a fourth section headed "external involvement". Each executive must now list objectives for personal/civic and community activity—he or she knows that we regard this as an important part of the job.[8]

Some employers have established partnerships with local schools in an effort to raise the quality of education received by youth who may otherwise tend to become an increasingly disadvantaged work force.[9] In other communities groups of businesses together, and on occasion with universities and labor organizations, have developed partnerships and programs for measurable goals for progress in the schools, summer jobs, part-time employment for high school students, and entry-level jobs for graduates.

The illustrations introduced above of unions engaged in various community functions, beyond the immediate benefit of their membership, and the activities of profit-making business enterprises directed to public purposes beyond the traditional patterns presumed to benefit stockholders both suggest difficult and fundamental issues of the demarcation of private and public purposes in American society.[10] The illustrations suggest that the provision of collective-type goods and services in a society, often identified as the sphere of government alone, may also be met by labor unions (or other nonprofit organizations), even by profit-making business enterprises, or by various forms of joint organizations and partnerships, as well as by governments. In these circumstances, where is the dividing line between the public sector and the private sector? And what is the appropriate scope of activities of labor organizations, business enterprises, and governments? How is one to appraise the projects of various forms of partnerships or comingling of private and public functions?[11] How is efficiency to be identified?

These issues may be fruitfully considered in the setting of more detail on specific activities and programs that reflect the third method of labor organizations: the method of voluntary service to the community.

Labor and Community Service Organizations

The AFL-CIO has entered into continuing formal memoranda of understanding with the United Way and the Red Cross nationally to provide for policies and procedures to govern their "cooperative" activities and "partnership in action." These activities are premised on the principles that "the union member is first and foremost a citizen of his community" and that "union members have a responsibility to their community."

The April 4, 1979, memorandum with the United Way formalizing a collaborative and special relationship that had existed for more than thirty years, begins with a statement of common principles: "voluntarism is the essence of a democratic society"; "the government's fundamental responsibility in meeting the basic health and welfare needs of the American people can best be discharged in cooperation with voluntary agencies"; and "voluntary associations of free men and women must pioneer in new directions to meet the changing needs of our times."[12]

Through its Department of Community Services, the AFL-CIO encourages its members and other unions to develop and maintain a mutually satisfactory cooperative relationship with the United Way through labor participation in fund raising, program development, policy formulation, allocations, volunteer efforts, and community planning. The United Way "affirms its support of the declared public policy of the United States, and respects the rights of its employees to join organizations of their own choosing for the purpose of collective bargaining in good faith and for grievance purposes, if that is their desire." The United Way will continue to purchase union-made goods and services whenever reasonably available.

The memorandum also provides for a detailed role of union representatives in the structure of the United Way. The AFL-CIO will be "adequately represented" on the United Way board, its executive committee and other committees, and in officer positions. There will be a Labor Participation Department with a full-time labor director and staff nominated by the AFL-CIO Department of Community Services. The memorandum also provides for detailed consultation on programs before implementation, including an annual joint work plan.

There are currently more than 350 full-time labor representatives on the staff and payroll of the United Way around the country engaged in solicitation of funds from employees, program development, allocation among agencies, and community planning. There have been developed model memoranda of understanding to be executed between state federations of labor and central labor councils and a state or a local United Way organization modeled on the national arrangement.

Employee contributions, both union members and nonmembers, account for approximately two-thirds of the funds that United Ways raise each year. Approximately 200 full-time state and local AFL-CIO community services liaisons serve as links between their central labor bodies and United Ways in 155 communities. A major activity of the AFL-CIO Community Services Program is to recruit, train, and place members from organized labor on the decision-making bodies of health, welfare, and human service organizations.

There have been difficulties in some communities over the interference of "antiunion forces" with the rights of employees of United Way agencies to join unions.[13] The Federation has proposed that the 1979 memorandum of agreement with the United Way be extended to all local agencies' applicants for United Way funding as a condition precedent to such grants.

A union counseling program is conducted nationwide under the auspices of central labor bodies and in cooperation with United Ways. It trains rank-and-file union members in providing information to members in need and in referring them to appropriate service agencies in their community. Seminars are held for people planning to retire or those recently retired. Seminars are also conducted on services to the unemployed outlining programs and resources available and how to secure them through a cooperative program with the National Association of Letter Carriers and the U.S. Postal Service. Letter carriers watch for signs, such as an unusual accumulation of mail, indicating that a person may be in trouble and refer the name to community service agencies.[14]

The American Red Cross and the AFL-CIO through its Department of Community Services entered into a Memorandum of Understanding on May 5, 1982, somewhat analogous to that with the United Way: "Organized labor can assist Red Cross Services in three ways: by contributing funds; by performing volunteer services; and by participating in policy making, planning and administration of Red Cross Services through their membership on Red Cross boards and committees." In turn, "the Red Cross can help organized labor by making its basic services—for the members of the armed forces and veterans and in the areas of disaster, blood, safety education, and nursing—readily available to working Americans on the basis of need."[15]

The memorandum provides for continuing labor participation in existing services such as blood services, disaster services, and first aid training and for the development and promotion of union counseling in all Red Cross services and in experimental projects and programs. Liaison representations will be selected by mutual agreement to serve on the Red Cross staff.

The memorandum includes the following section on collective bargaining;

a. American Red Cross Collective Bargaining Policy

The American Red Cross supports the rights of employees to choose or refuse to choose union representation and to do so in an environment that preserves freedom of choice. Where Red Cross employees have freely elected collective representation in units appropriate for collective bargaining, the American Red Cross endorses fully the mutual obligation of the Red Cross employers and employee representatives to bargain in good faith with respect to wages, hours, and other terms and conditions of employment toward a just contractual settlement and to do so consistent with the overriding necessity of preserving the continuity of Red Cross services essential to life, health, and public well-being.

b. AFL-CIO Statement on Union Recognition and Collective Bargaining.

It is the position of the AFL-CIO that all employees of the Red Cross have the right to join unions of their own choosing for collective bargaining purposes and for handling grievances. It is the position of the AFL-CIO that the Red Cross management should respect the right of their employees, to join unions of their own choosing and should bargain in good faith with these unions on wages, hours, and conditions of employment.

While the AFL-CIO welcomes the progress made in this direction by the Red Cross, it nevertheless recognizes that there are a number of differences in approach. However, both parties to this agreement pledge themselves to cooperate with one another in resolving themselves to cooperate with one another in resolving these differences on a case-by-case basis, taking into consideration the interests of the employees, the employers, and the total community—which in the long run, are one and the same.

Bricklayers and Laborers Nonprofit Housing Company

The Federation and the Building and Construction Trades Department have sought to stimulate the investment of pension funds developed under collective bargaining agreement into housing for medium- and low-income persons. The purposes have been to provide more housing units, constructed by union labor and contractors, while yielding a satisfactory rate of return to the pension fund. In November 1964 the AFL-CIO created its Mortgage Investment Trust. The major thrust of this activity has been government-guaranteed construction loans for multifamily apartment projects and nursing homes.

In 1983 the AFL-CIO sponsored another Housing Investment Trust with emphasis on permanent mortgage financing for single-family-home mortgages. The Housing Investment Trust functions under the control of a joint labor-management board with a chairman with experience in the U.S. Department of Housing and Urban Affairs.

In Boston, the Bricklayers and Laborers unions, under the leadership of Thomas McIntyre, vice-president of the International Union of Bricklayers and Allied Craftsmen, created the Nonprofit Housing Company. The city of Boston contributed the land but will collect taxes it did not previously receive; financing costs were kept low by leveraging union pension funds into a construction loan; the pension funds were not invested as equity in the project and were never at risk. The single-family brick rowhouses of 1,100 square feet were sold for about $70,000 each, 50 percent below the market price of comparable units, by lottery to moderate- and low-income buyers whose average income was $27,000 and who were long-term residents of the neighborhood.

The purpose of the Nonprofit Housing Company, according to Thomas McIntyre, is to show "that unions are a force for good in the community."[16]

Labor and Health Care Coalitions

In the late 1970s and early 1980s health care coalitions emerged in a number of cities. The rapid inflation in health insurance costs, the growing appreciation in the labor-management[17] and the business community of the structural issues in health, and the decline in federal support for health planning organizations contributed to the development of community coalitions, often initiated by business companies and expanded to include doctors, hospitals, Blue Cross and Blue Shield and insurance companies, and labor organizations. On occasion local governments are also represented.

Labor unions were initially reticent to join such community groups since many union leaders were committed to pursue health care objectives through collective bargaining or by the legislative achievement of national health insurance. Many businesses in the early 1980s could only propose to contain costs by more co-payments and higher deductibles in the calculation of benefits. After the formation of the Group of Six in 1980—a national coalition the AFL-CIO joined on the condition that its advocacy for national health insurance was understood (the other members are American Hospital Association, American Medical Association, Blue Cross and Blue Shield Association, the Business Roundtable, and Health Insurance Association of America)—labor organizations joined local coalitions more frequently. Moreover, the Johnson Foundation grants to local coalitions to develop means of restraining the rate of health care cost increases encouraged labor union participation, and labor is represented in all of the eleven communities with these

Table 7–1
Composition of Local Health Care Coalitions, 1988

Composition	Number of Coalitions with Representatives	Percentage of Total
Business	114	94.2
Business only	5	4.1
Hospitals/associations	98	81.0
Physicians/medical societies	94	77.7
Blue Cross and Blue Shield	79	65.3
Commercial insurers	75	62.0
Labor organizations	50	41.3
All six constituents	27	22.3

grants. Table 7–1 shows the composition of 121 health care coalitions in 1988.

The most important activities reported by these coalitions were ranked according to the frequency that coalitions in 1988 said they engaged in the activity:

Education of members, 106 (87.6 percent)

Benefit design, 95 (78.5 percent)

Legislative advocacy, 79 (65.3 percent)

Database, 78 (64.5 percent)

Legislative analysis, 73 (60.3 percent)

Health promotion/wellness, 45 (37.3 percent)

Utilization management, 54 (44.6 percent)

The largest number of coalitions are found in communities in the East North Central (eighteen), the South Atlantic (eighteen), Middle Atlantic (fifteen) and Pacific states (twelve).

While the country confronts significant national health care problems,[18] such as access to care for the uninsured, cost inflation, and quality of care, it is also apparent that there are significant differences among communities in types of hospitals and capacity, utilization rates, practice patterns among physicians and their numbers, the characteristics of the population to be served, benefit levels and the uninsured, the role of local governments and the political leadership, and others. These factors among others warrant the discussion of the facts of health care and its costs on a community basis among the diverse groups represented in a coalition.

Local coalitions differ a great deal in the extent to which they have an influence on the health care system. At a minimum, the representatives of the major organizations in health care meet and learn something of each other and disseminate statistical data on performance costs and behavior. Some coalitions penetrate deeper and develop programs to influence hospital utilization, ambulatory care, case management, and benefit designs. A few may go further and organize alternative delivery systems such as HMOs (health maintenance organizations) or PPOs (preferred provider organizations) to furnish health services on a capitation basis or at a discount from prevailing rates or fees. A few other coalitions may undertake special projects, such as care for the uninsured, consolidation of hospital facilities, or seeking relief from the high cost of professional liability.

Boston Compact

The object of the Boston Compact is to improve public education in the schools. Boston business, university, and union leaders have signed separate agreements with the public schools establishing measurable goals for progress in the schools, youth employment, and higher education.[19]

The background to the compact includes a decade of partnerships between individual public schools and businesses and universities. Boston was also the site for a major demonstration project under the 1977 Youth Employment and Demonstration Projects Act. Some 4,000 low-income young people were guaranteed part-time jobs if they remained in school. The program taught city and school officials the necessity of working together. In the early 1980s Boston business leaders agreed to organize jobs for public school students and with the school system build a bridge from school to work: summer jobs, part-time employment for high school students, and entry-level jobs for graduates.

The organization linking the business community and the schools is the Boston Private Industry Council authorized by the Job Training Partnership Act (1978 and 1982). The members are business executives, the school superintendent, a university president, and community-based organizations. The business community has provided funds for innovative teaching and programs in the schools, including counseling and financial help to prospective college students. The universities calculate they contribute about $7 million a year to the compact—half in services and half in scholarships.

By 1987, the Boston graduating class was 48 percent black, 31 percent white, and 11 percent Hispanic and largely from low-income households. Graduate placements were more than a thousand, and nearly 700 companies provided more than 3,000 summer jobs. The Boston Area Building Trades Union Agreement with the school system has led to an increase in the number of high school graduates going into apprenticeship programs. "But the school system has a long way to go. Of those in the class of 1986, 46 percent dropped out. And 64 percent of the seniors at district and magnet schools score at 40 percent or lower on national reading tests."[20]

In a number of other communities, some employers are establishing partnerships with the public schools to raise the quality of education and the skills received by potential employees.[21] Save for apprenticeship programs and teacher organizations, unions have infrequently been involved.

Professionalization of Teaching:
Dade County, Florida

Public sector labor organizations and employers have a special opportunity to affect the community and community views of unions. They interact directly with the public in a variety of ways. They influence the community perception of the quality of service, and they reflect the concerns of public employees for dedicated performance and sensitivity to professional standards and efficiency. Public employees are in a distinctive position to be involved in community service. One illustration is provided by the United Teachers of Dade (American Federation of Teachers) in cooperation with the Dade County Public Schools, moving beyond a conventional collective bargaining relationship in the fourth largest school district in the country, with multiracial and new immigrant problems.

In the early 1970s the first agreement provided for a series of joint labor-management task forces to address mutual issues and concerns. From these discussions emerged teacher-faculty councils at each school site to serve as advisory to principals. A Quality Instruction Incentives program emerged that led in 1985 to a joint Professionalization of Teaching Task Force to meet the challenges of educational reform. In 1988, thirty-three schools were involved in a nationally recognized School-Based Management/Shared Decision-Making experiment, which encourages school-site and problem-solving creativity by teachers and administrators. Twelve additional schools are involved in the collaborative Partners in Education project, which includes an added dimension of parent, business, and community input into the operation and oversight of their schools. Satellite learning centers have been established that are the nation's first public schools at the workplace.

These joint activities developed by the parties to the collective agreement have been very well received in the larger community—among parents, business leaders, and community organizations who are involved in the "Renaissance in Education" in Dade County. A major bond issue was readily approved by the voters, and the direct influence of the union and the school board and superintendent of schools is reflected outside the classroom into the community.[22]

Questions

1. Does the labor movement devote too much time and energy to community service organizations, such as the United Way and the Red Cross, or not enough? What is the rationale for such activity? Is it possible to estimate its impact on the trade union movement or on the community?

2. Compare the AFL-CIO and the Red Cross statements on "Union Recognition and Collective Bargaining" and "Collective Bargaining Policy." In what respects and in what circumstances are they at odds? What role do these formal agreements serve?

3. What are the favorable and unfavorable consequences to the union movement involvement with a number of other groups in a community program such as the United Way, a health care coalition, or an education program?

4. Why have unions, businesses, and other groups gone into community activities illustrated in this chapter? Would it be better to let government do such work?

5. Do these activities take away from higher-priority programs to which scarce leadership, manpower, and funds should better be applied?

Notes

1. Sidney Webb and Beatrice Webb, *Industrial Democracy* (London: Longmans, Green, 1914; first published in 1897), p. 150, pt. II. Beatrice Potter (Mrs. Sidney Webb) coined the phrase *collective bargaining* in the current meaning. (See p. 173, note 1.) Also see Margaret Cole, *Beatrice Webb* (New York: Harcourt, Brace, 1946), pp. 34–44, 73–83.

2. See James B. Kennedy, *Beneficiary Features of American Trade Unions* (Baltimore: Johns Hopkins Press, 1908).

3. Derek C. Bok and John T. Dunlop, *Labor and the American Community* (New York: Simon & Shuster, 1970), pp. 375–379.

4. *Proceedings of the Eighth Constitutional Convention of the AFL-CIO*, Atlantic City, N.J., October 2–7, 1969, 1:544–545.

5. AFL-CIO, Executive Council, "Community Service Agencies in the Private Sector," February 20, 1981. These views were also incorporated in a 1968 resolution of the executive council.

6. Harvard George S. Dively Award for Corporate Public Initiative, John F. Kennedy School of Government, Harvard University.

7. "Corporate Social Responsibility" (remarks by John F. Akers, president and chief executive officer, IBM, on the occasion of the granting of the first Harvard George S. Dively Award for Corporate Public Initiative to International Business Ma-

chine Corporation, February 4, 1986, John F. Kennedy School of Government, Harvard University).

8. The Harvard George S. Dively Award for Corporate Public Initiative, was presented to General Mills in 1987. It was accepted by H. B. Atwater, Jr., chairman and chief executive officer, on November 16, 1987.

9. "Employers Work with Schools to Ensure Educated Workforce," Bureau of National Affairs, *Daily Labor Report,* September 9, 1988, pp. A2–4.

10. See Thomas K. McCraw, "The Historical Background," in *American Society: Public and Private Responsibilities,* ed. Winthrop Knowlton and Richard Zeckhauser (Cambridge, Mass: Ballinger, 1986), pp. 15–42.

11. See Burton A. Weisbrod, *The Voluntary Nonprofit Sector: An Economic Analysis* (Lexington, Mass: Lexington Books, 1977).

12. *A Cooperative Memorandum of the Understanding between the United Way of America and the AFL-CIO* (Washington, D.C: Department of Community Services, AFL-CIO, April 4, 1979). Also see *Proceedings of the Thirteenth Constitutional Convention of the AFL-CIO,* Washington, D.C., November 15–20, 1979, pp. 233–334.

13. AFL-CIO, Executive Council, "Community Service Agencies."

14. See *Labor and United Way: Working for a Better Community, Labor's Community Services Liaison Program* (Washington, D.C.: AFL-CIO, 1985).

15. *Memorandum of Understanding between American Red Cross and the AFL-CIO Department of Community Services* (Washington, D.C.: AFL-CIO, 1982).

16. Sherrie Hannan, "Boston Unions Build Affordable Housing," *Network Builder, Chicago Rehab Network Newsletter* (August–September 1987); *Boston Globe,* January 11, 1986, p. 37.

17. See Labor-Management Group, *Position Papers on Health Care Costs* (Washington, D.C.: AFL-CIO and The Business Roundtable, 1978).

18. See Labor-Management Group, *Policy Issues in Health Care and Six Case Studies* (Washington, D.C.: AFL-CIO and The Business Roundtable, 1987).

19. William J. Spring, "Youth Unemployment and the Transition from School to Work: Programs in Boston, Frankfurt, and London," *New England Economic Review* (March–April 1987): 3–16.

20. William Spring, "Students and Jobs," *Boston Globe,* April 25, 1988, p. 19

21. Bureau of National Affairs, *Daily Labor Reports,* September 9, 1988, pp. A-2 to A-4.

22. Dade County Public Schools and the United Teachers of Dade, *Renaissance in Education* (1988); Professionalization of Teaching Task Force, *Blueprint to Professionalization of Teaching/Education,* January 25, 1989. (Miami, Florida, Joint Publications of the Dade County Public Schools and the United Teachers of Dade).

8
The Philosophy of the American Labor Movement

The purposes, objectives, and longer-term aspirations of a labor movement reflect its constituencies and national environment just as they also help to shape its course. Labor organizations that grew up in the last half of the nineteenth and early twentieth centuries in the New World, with a significant influx of workers with attachments to unions and political parties in the old country, struggled with alternative policies toward employers, the political process, and political parties, toward other labor organizations and producers, as well as with alternative roles for the working class and the vision of their role in the larger society.

The AFL and its constituents from the outset in the 1880s were courted by a wide range of philosophies. The Socialists and Social Democrats claimed a special relationship to the labor movement,[1] and they were capable of mustering as much as 40 percent of the votes in the AFL conventions for a number of years.[2] The syndicalists, the anarchists, and later the Communist party sought to infiltrate and to capture the mainstream of the American labor movement.[3] The 1930s saw the flourishing of philosophical and political factions in the economic crisis of the Great Depression, the shifting international scene, and the initial rise of CIO unions. The period reflected, particularly in cities such as Detroit, New York, and San Francisco, the ferment and appeal of the Communists, Socialists of various persuasions, Trotskyites, Lovestonites, and a variety of liberal persuasions advocating a new role for government in the Roosevelt era.[4]

From the outset leaders of the Federation have sought to articulate a philosophy that coalesced the diverse membership, that provided a vision for working men and women, and that was somewhat compatible with the larger society. For analytical purposes, the term *philosophy* is used to encompass the following array of orientations and perspectives: attitudes toward capitalism, relationships to the major political parties and to the ideological left, support and affiliation with international labor organizations comprised of labor movements of various countries, the roles assigned to legislation and to collective bargaining, and the objectives of the labor organization and its place envisaged in American society.

This chapter provides excerpts from constitutions of labor organizations and statements by leaders of the Federation over the past seventy-five years so that their views as to the purposes and aspirations of the American labor movement may be expressed in their own words. These quotations also reflect the changing formulation of the objectives of labor unions and their relationships to the larger American society.

Preambles of the Constitutions

AFL Constitution (1886)

Whereas, a struggle is going on in all the nations of the civilized world between the oppressors and the oppressed of all countries, a struggle between the capitalist and the laborer, which grows in intensity from year to year, and will work disastrous results to the toiling millions if they are not combined for mutual protection and benefit;

It, therefore, behooves the representatives of the trade and labor unions of America, in convention assembled, to adopt such measures and disseminate such principles among the mechanics and laborers of our country as will permanently unite them to secure the recognition of rights to which they are justly entitled.

We, therefore, declare ourselves in favor of the formation of a thorough federation, embracing every trade and labor organization in America, organized under the trade union system.

CIO Constitution (1938)

The Congress of Industrial Organizations grew out of the needs of the unorganized workers of America which could be met most effectively by the industrial form of organization. Since its formation in 1935, the CIO has grown because the service it has given to American workers has made ours a better America. We of the CIO are the sons and daughters of ancestors who came to America to escape absolutism in government, bigotry in religion, and economic exploitation. We of the CIO are proud of this American quest for liberty and the struggle for equality. We seek, today, to implement this great heritage. We are dedicated to the responsibility for furthering economic opportunity, religious freedom, and political participation.

Democracy stems entirely from free choice. Diligently practiced, it is the only logical human formula for the attainment of economic and political independence, for the realization of a just and equitable return on one's labor, for guarantees of full employment, of social security, and of the protection of the family as an institution.

In the achievement of this task we turn to the people because we have faith in them; and we oppose all those who would violate this American emphasis of responsibility for human dignity, all those who would use power to exploit the people in the interest of alien loyalties.

The struggle for human freedom is a continuous one. The task of those who would bring security and greater understanding to America and throughout the world is endless. It is in this all-consuming struggle, however, that men and organizations make their contributions to a better life.

Therefore, we in the CIO glory in our heritage and in the hope of our future. Racial persecution, intolerance, selfishness, and greed have no place in the human family. We will not be satisfied until ours is a world of free men and women and of happy children. It's to these ends that this Constitution of the CIO is dedicated. It is the charter of our lives; through it we seek to maintain and extend liberty and opportunity here and throughout the world.

Order of the Knights of Labor of America (1878–1885)

The alarming development and aggressiveness of great capitalists and corporations, unless checked, will inevitably lead to the pauperization and hopeless degradation of the toiling masses.

It is imperative, if we desire to enjoy the full blessings of life, that a check be placed upon unjust accumulation, and the power for evil of aggregated wealth.

This much-desired object can be accomplished only by the united efforts of those who obey the divine injunction, "In the sweat of thy face shalt thou eat bread."

Therefore we have formed the Order of Knights of Labor, for the purpose of organizing and directing the power of the industrial masses, not as a political party, for it is more—in it are crystallized sentiments and measures for the benefit of whole people, but it should be borne in mind, when exercising the right of suffrage, that most of the objects herein set forth can only be obtained through legislation, and that it is the duty of all to assist in nominating and supporting with their votes only such candidates as will pledge their support to those measures, regardless of party. But no one shall, however, be compelled to vote with the majority; and calling upon all who believe in securing "the greatest good to the greatest number", to join and assist us, we declare to the world that our aims are:

I. To make industrial and moral worth, not wealth, the true standard of individual and National greatness.

II. To secure to the workers the full enjoyment of the wealth they create, sufficient leisure in which to develop their intellectual, moral and social faculties; all of the benefits, recreation and pleasures of association; in a word, to enable them to share in the gains and honors of advancing civilization.

Industrial Workers of the World (1907)

The working class and the employing class have nothing in common. There can be no peace so long as hunger and want are found among millions of the working people and the few, who make up the employing class, have all the good things of life.

Between these two classes a struggle must go on until the workers of the world organize as a class, take possession of the earth and the machinery of production, and abolish the wage system.

We find that the centering of the management of industries into fewer and fewer hands makes the trade unions unable to cope with the ever-growing power of the employing class. The trade unions foster a state of affairs which allows one set of workers to be pitted against another set of workers in the same industry, thereby helping defeat one another in wage wars. Moreover, the trade unions aid the employing class to mislead the workers into the belief that the working class have interests in common with their employers.

These conditions can be changed and the interest of the working class upheld only by an organization formed in such a way that all its members in any one industry, or in all industries if necessary, cease work whenever a strike or lockout is on in any department thereof, thus making an injury to one an injury to all.

Instead of the conservative motto: "A fair day's wage for a fair day's work," we must inscribe on our banner the revolutionary watchword, "Abolition of the wage system."

It is the historic mission of the working class to do away with capitalism. The army of production must be organized, not only for the everyday struggle with capitalists, but also to carry on production when capitalism shall have been overthrown. By organizing industrially we are forming the structure of the new society within the shell of the old.

Knowing, therefore, that such an organization is absolutely necessary for our emancipation, we unite under the following constitution.

Samuel Gompers and Morris Hillquit: Socialism and Trade-Unionism (1914)

Mr. Hillquit: Then inform me on this: In its practical work in the labor movement is the American Federation of Labor guided by a general social philosophy, or is it not?

Mr. Gompers: It is guided by the history of the past, drawing its lessons from history. It knows the conditions by which the working people are surrounded. It works along the line of least resistance and endeavors to accomplish the best results in improving the condition of the working people, men, women and children, to-day and to-morrow—and to-morrow's to-morrow and each day, making it a better day than the one that had gone before. The guiding principle, philosophy and aim of the labor movement is to secure a better life for all.

Mr. Hillquit: But in these efforts to improve conditions from day to day, you must have an underlying standard of what is better, don't you?

Mr. Gompers: No. You start out with a given program, and everything must conform to it; and if the facts do not conform to your theories, then your actions betray the state of mind "so much the worse for the facts."

Mr. Hillquit: Mr. Gompers, what I ask you is this: You say you try to make the conditions of the workers better every day. In order to determine whether conditions are better or worse, you must have some standards by which you distinguish the bad from the good in the labor movement, must you not?

Mr. Gompers: Certainly. Does it require much discernment to know that a wage of $3.00 a workday of 8 hours a day in sanitary workshops are all better than $2.50 and 12 hours a day under perilous conditions of labor? It does not require much conception of a social philosophy to understand that.

Mr. Hillquit: Then, Mr. Gompers, by parity of reasoning, $4.00 a day and 7 hours of work, and truly attractive working conditions are still better?

Mr. Gompers: Unquestionably.

Mr. Hillquit: Therefore,

Mr. Gompers: (interrupting): Just a moment. I have not stipulated $4.00 a day or $8.00 a day or any number of dollars a day or 7 hours a day or any number of hours a day. The aim is to secure the best conditions obtainable for the workers.

Mr. Hillquit: Yes; and when these conditions are obtained—

Mr. Gompers: (interrupting): Why, then we want better—

Mr. Hillquit: (continuing): You will still strive for better?

Mr. Gompers: Yes.

Mr. Hillquit: Now, my question is, will this effort on the part of organized labor ever stop before the workers receive the full reward for their labor?

Mr. Gompers: It won't stop at all at any particular point, whether it be that towards which you have just stated, or anything else. The working people will never stop in their effort to obtain a better life for themselves, and for their wives and for their children and for humanity.

Mr. Hillquit: Then the object of the organized workmen is to obtain complete social justice for themselves and for their wives and for their children?

Mr. Gompers: (interrupting): Every day. That does not limit it.

Mr. Hillquit: Until such time—

Mr. Gompers: (interrupting): Not until any time.

Mr. Hillquit: In other words

Mr. Gompers: (interrupting): In other words, we go farther than you. You have an end; we have not.[5]

George Meany, "What Labor Means by 'More'"

To put aside the pressing problems of the day [in 1955] and to speculate about the America of 1980 is a challenging exercise of the imagination. Given the fabulous inventiveness of our country, and the promises of technology, the America of 1980 might be even more unrecognizable to us today than is the America of 25 years ago. But without world peace as a foundation of the future, rational predictions about the next quarter-century are utterly impossible. Moreover, advances in technology alone do not and cannot solve the great questions of social arrangements and social justice. These are questions not of technology but of morals, not of science but of wisdom.

Plain realism dictates, therefore, that our thinking about the America of the quarter-century ahead must be limited to goals rather than to predictions. Yet long-range goals, if they are meaningful, originate in the world of today, and are shaped by one's tradition, and one's philosophy. In a single man's lifetime, twenty-five years is a long time, perhaps half the span of his mature, vigorous life. Institutions, and the men who reflect them, have a longer perspective than individuals alone, and in the A.F. of L. our traditions and our philosophy have emerged from an experience of seventy-five years. Our goals can be understood only in terms of that experience. Moreover, the goals of a future but a quarter of century away will not appear so unreal when measured against a philosophy hammered out by millions of Americans over the course of three-quarters of a century.

Our goals as trade-unionists are modest, for we do not seek to recast American society in any particular doctrinaire or ideological image. We seek an ever rising standard of living. Sam Gompers once put the matter succinctly. When asked what the labor movement wanted, he answered "More." If by a better standard of living we mean not only more money but more leisure and a richer cultural life, the answer remains, "More."

But how do we get "more"? Imperfect in many details as our system may be, this country has adopted a flexible method for increasing the standard of living while maintaining freedom. It is the method of voluntary collective bargaining of free decision making outside the coercions of government, in the solution of economic disagreement. And it is through the give-and-take of collective bargaining that we seek to achieve our goals.

When Freemen Bargain . . .

Collective bargaining, we have learned, can exist only in the environment of political freedom. Where there is no individual liberty, there is no free trade-union movement either. Every dictator, from left to right, as a first step in the consolidation of power has sought to destroy free trade unions. And so we are dedicated to freedom, not only political but also economic, through a system of private enterprise. We believe in the American profit system. We believe in free competition. The American private-enterprise system, despite some defects, has achieved far greater results for wage earners than any other social system in history. The American worker, without doubt, is the best-paid, best-clothed, and best-housed worker in the world. But he can and should be much better paid, better clothed, and better housed in 1980. The children of American workers have greater educational opportunities than children of any other workers; the workers' wives and families have greater comforts and opportunities for social and cultural development than families of workers in any other land. These comforts and opportunities, too, can be greatly increased over the next quarter-century.

We are proud, understandably, of the contribution of trade-unionism to the changing American private-enterprise system. Certainly we have differed with our employers over the sharing of the benefits—this is the heart of bargaining—and we shall differ again during the next quarter century. But throughout we have relied upon the judgement of free men, unimpeded by the interference of government, to reach private agreement, and it is certainly the hope and resolve of the A.F. of L. that our differences shall continue to be settled in this way.

On its philosophical side, collective bargaining is a means of assuring justice and fair treatment. In the economic realm it is a means of prodding management to increase efficiency and output, and of placing upon trade unions great responsibilities to limit their demands to practical realities. A failure to recognize the unique role of collective bargaining is a failure to understand the distinctive new nature of American private enterprise as it has evolved over the past seventy-five years.

The Rights of Management

Are we likely, by 1980, to reach the limits of collective bargaining? For the A.F. of L., I can say flatly that collective bargaining is not a means of seeking a voice in management. We do not want so-called "codetermination"—the representation of unions on the board of directors or in the active management of a company. In Germany, where trade unions have endorsed such a plan, codetermination emerges from a peculiar background—the political use of corporate power by cartel management. And in that country it has some logic as a means of maintaining economic democracy. Here in the U.S., with a different background and tradition, with a different kind of management, with the acceptance of collective bargaining, codetermination has no reality. To some in management, any limitation of management's right to set the conditions of work is a challenge to its integrity. But this point of view is diminishing. I would expect that by 1980 it will have disappeared completely.

There remains the more concrete and difficult question of where a line can be drawn. In recent years certainly the scope of collective bargaining has expanded considerably. Where once it included largely wages, hours, and maintenance of health and safety conditions, and, later, hiring, firing, and promotion, it now includes medical care, pensions, and the like. Today labor is beginning to question the unilateral right of management to set production standards and even (as in the recent hatters' strike in Norwalk, Connecticut) to stipulate the location of plant.

While exact answers are hard to give, a general principle can be established: A union exists to protect the livelihood and interests of a worker. Those matters that do not touch a worker directly, a union cannot and will not challenge. These may include investment policy, a decision to make a new product, a desire to erect a new plant so as to be closer to expanding markets, to re-invest out of earnings or seek new equity capital, etc. But where management decisions affect a worker directly a union will intervene. When a company, for example, renounces union standards, and arbitrarily disrupts the lives of thousands of workers because it may save 7 cents a hat, a union will resist. If trade unions in 1980 are not willing to resist such efforts, they will not have—and would not deserve—the kind of influence they hold in the U.S. in 1955. . . .

Who's Afraid of Automation?

In the next twenty-five years the flexibility of collective bargaining will meet its severest test in the rapid changes in the technological structure of industry and the consequent wholesale changes in the character of the labor force. This problem is symbolized by the term automation. By 1980 we may have completely "automatic" factories, run by electronically set devices without the intervention of human hand. But we know from experience that progress in technology does not occur in large, magical jumps, but grows out of past advances. Similarly the attendant problems of adapting to progress do not change basically; they simply appear larger and more complex. Our concern, thus, is less with 1980 than with the road to it.

Certainly the trade-union movement does not oppose technological change. There can be no turning back to a negative or short-sighted policy of limiting progress. (During the depression someone half seriously proposed a five-year moratorium on new inventions.) The answer to technological change lies in smoothing its transitions and cushioning the shocks that attend it. This means, in the immediate sense, the establishment of severance pay, retraining of skills, reorganization of work schedules. These are social costs that industry will have to bear in order to avoid the wasting of human resources—and to avoid our calling on government to bear these costs if industry fails to do so. . . .

The Hand of Government

The A.F. of L. is primarily an economic organization, seeking its ends in the economic field. In recent years we have been involved with government. Whether we shall continue to be so involved in the next twenty-five years depends in large measure on industry. Only when industry has failed to accept social responsibility has labor, along with the people as a whole, turned to government for help. There is always the danger that concentration of power may whittle away individual freedoms. In fact, the heavy hand of government in the past has throttled freedom for private collective enterprise. But government has an obligation to help people do what they cannot do for themselves.

The A.F. of L., for example, at one time opposed a government system of social security. We felt that through private collective bargaining wages could be raised high enough for the individual to accumulate his own savings, or pay for his own annuity, thus assuring himself security. But the depression of the 1930's changed our thinking. When savings were wiped out and families and individuals had to go on relief for lack of unemployment insurance, we accepted the principle of government social security. We still believe that government alone should not be called upon to provide complete social security. The inadequacies of the government system give unionists an added incentive to press for realistic security through private health, welfare, and pension plans. Collective bargaining, not government, must ultimately provide the necessary protection against the deficiencies of the economic system. . . .

In Politics to Stay

But we shall remain in politics. The fact that we do so does not mean that the A.F. of L. will be tied to any political party. Nor does it close off any particular road in politics. I do not think the membership of the A.F. of L. is thinking now in terms of a national political party sponsored by labor. Yet if the action of the two major parties leaves us no alternative in our efforts to safeguard and raise the living standards of the workers, labor will go as far as it must down that political road.

This stand does not preclude labor's support of Republican candidates. Although the A.F. of L. endorsed the Democratic candidate for President in 1952 and has generally found itself in sympathy with more Democratic congressional candidates than Republican, it has actually supported a number of Republican candidates both for Congress and for state offices. Certainly, if one looks at American politics in historical perspective, and notes the shift in thinking of sections of the Republican party, one finds more areas of political agreement among the bulk of voters regarding major domestic programs than there were twenty-five years ago. And probably more areas of common agreement than disagreement. But differences do exist. Our sole principle has been, is, and will be to seek the election—without regard to party labels—of those who believe as we do in an economic system based on prosperity at the lower rungs of the economic ladder, and to oppose those who hold otherwise.

Better America, Better World

As America looks forward to 1980 there could be no goal more worthy than demonstrating to the world moral leadership. Sharing our wealth and the methods by which we create it is but an act of humanitarianism. Proof by demonstration of our adherence to principles of morality is the test of America's sincerity as a member of the world family of nations.

For example, here at home we must speed up progress toward wiping out racialism in all its forms and colors. Man—made in the image of God—has no particular kind of color, hair, or facial structure. Until our actions—not merely our words—demonstrate that America will not tolerate racialism, we cannot adequately provide the moral leadership that the free world so sorely needs.

Of all the people on earth we in America have the greatest opportunity to make the future measure up to the highest ideals of mankind. The voluntary cooperation of labor and management in a free society can carry us far toward the attainment of this goal for all people. The obstructions in the path to cooperation are not insurmountable. There is but a minority of employers who need drop their antagonism to the right of free men to choose trade-unionism as a way of life. Then, as truly free men, labor and management may join in a constructive effort to lay down simple rules of decency and unite in promoting mutual advances.

The American Federation of Labor stands today for the same ideals and principles that have proved to be sound and constructive during all its past years. We have never lost faith in the United States of America and its Constitution dedicated to human liberty. In the light of that continuing faith, we not only expect America to lead the way for millions of people literally hungry for freedom and democracy, but we also expect that years ahead will bring a better and even better America.[6]

Contrasting Statements of Purpose

Dave Beck, former president of the Teamsters

Members join our union for only one purpose; to sell their labor for the highest price they can get. . . . This international union and its various subdivisions, its local unions—is the machinery of our people to sell that labor.[7]

*Walter Reuther, former president of the United
Automobile Workers and former president of the CIO*

. . . It was inevitable in early days of unionism, since there was so much to be done in the matter of improving living and working standards, that the labor movement would be devoted almost exclusively to those things. In its next phase, as I've said, these things will be deemphasized—not neglected—and the unions will take on the broader function of concern for the quality of our society as a whole. The labor movement will become less of an economic movement and more of a social movement. It will be concerned with the economic factors, of course, but also with the moral, the spiritual, the intellectual, and the social nature of our society, and all of this in terms of an ultimate objective—the fulfillment of the complete human being.[8]

Thomas R. Donahue, *The Labor Struggle: Reflections on The Encyclical of Pope John Paul II* (1982)

The U.S. Labor Movement in Struggle

To understand fully the new hope and new encouragement which this encyclical gives to the labor movement in the United States, one must see that movement, as it sees itself—facing the unrelenting opposition of the nation's employers to every single expression of desire on the part of workers to enjoy the "indispensable" union affiliation of which the Pope speaks.

In our system of labor relations, a union either exists or not at each workplace depending on the majority expression of the workers at that workplace. The union either enjoys "exclusive recognition" as the collective bargaining agent for a defined group of employees or it is not recognized at all.

This fact seems to have encouraged the view of U.S. employers that almost any tactic is permissible in their struggle to convince a majority of their employees that they don't need, or don't want, a union to represent them.

Consequently, our unions struggle every day for recognition, for their right to exist at a particular workplace or in a particular plant, hospital or establishment of whatever kind. The exercise by workers of their right to associate freely with one another is challenged by the employer as if the effort to assert that right could properly be treated as the subject of a contest, of a game. The workers who attempt to form or join a union are arrayed on one side with the employer on the other. The employer's advisers, the "labor-management consultants," mount a campaign of propaganda, pleas for loyalty to the employer, and often, intimidation and coercion. Arrayed on the other side are the union adherents, their professional staff and their campaign—intended to offset the employer's propaganda, to attract new adherents to the union cause and to minimize any intimidation or coercion.

The inevitable result of these struggles is the maintenance of a climate in which cooperation is difficult and coexistence is more the norm.

I do not claim that all virtue in such discussion and contest is on the union's side but only want to point out that what the Pope takes for granted as a right of association freely exercised, guaranteed in a democratic society, is often trampled upon in this country and others. And one must conclude that it is trampled upon in pursuit of the profit motive and in an effort to exclude workers from any voice in ownership, or management, or, indeed, from any effective participation in the fixing of the conditions under which they will labor.

The struggle of our unions is, as the Pope points out, a "struggle for the good which corresponds to the needs and merits of working people." We do not see it as a struggle against others but a struggle against their ignorance and their pursuit of the ultimate maximization of profit. It is never, for us, a struggle "for the sake of struggle" or "in order to eliminate an opponent," since the first is wasteful of human effort and the latter carries with it the elimination of the opportunity for employment—always too scarce in this country.

This part of the struggle can only end for us when our employers fully accept the teachings of the encyclical, and perceive the worker as a true partner in the process and not as some element of production to be managed, placated and supervised. That would require first and foremost, and at a minimum, absolute noninterference in a worker's choice to be represented by a union and a willingness to negotiate a fair contract in good faith.

U.S. Collective Bargaining System

The labor movement in this country has long insisted on a written collective bargaining agreement with each employer as the fundamental protection of workers on the job and has always regarded our collective bargaining system as the cornerstone of labor-management relations and, hopefully, as the basis for labor-management cooperation.

We believe in a conflict theory of collective bargaining as the soundest basis for worker representation, worker participation and worker gains, in the current labor-management climate, because we see no real or broad evidence of acceptance by employers of the concepts of just remuneration, protection of worker interests or of the participation of workers in the ownership, management or profits of the enterprise.

We accept fully the view that all capital is the product of past labor, that labor is not a commodity and that nothing has been created in the human realm except through labor. Consequently, we seek a redistribution of the wealth of our nation and an enlarged share in future wealth. Workers properly want, and are entitled to, a larger share of the wealth they produce. It is our almost universal experience that the employer—individual, corporate or non-profit organization (both secular and religious)—doesn't want to give workers their fair share, and we are therefore in essential conflict over this issue. It is, hopefully, a conflict which always "aims at the good of social justice."

Since our relationship with our employers remains at this primitive level of struggle, it has always been difficult for us to regard seriously, for ourselves, the forms of participation in the enterprise generally grouped under the heading of co-determination.

For so long as the attitudes of U.S. employers remain unchanged, we shall continue to advance a theory of collective bargaining rooted in the conflict between trade union efforts to advance social justice and what we regard as the employers' efforts to maximize profits and maintain "management prerogatives"—(a euphemism for unadulterated control of work rules or work process with the least possible "participation" of workers in management).

I would note, however, that we do believe that our adversarial role, appropriate to the conflict of collective bargaining, should be limited to the period of negotiation. During the lifetime of a contract so arrived at, it ought to be replaced by a period of cooperation aimed at maximizing the potential of the joint enterprise to advance the company's business and the workers' satisfaction.

For that reason and on that premise, many of our unions are participating in "labor-management committees" and other cooperative programs, where those programs have their base in collective bargaining. Much attention is now being paid to the question of worker satisfaction on the job and the quantity and quality of his or her work output. These two subjects have been joined under the title of "quality of worklife" and a great deal of experimentation is now going on, seeking to find new and better ways to give to workers a sense of pride in their work, a sense of their involvement in the production process, and through this sense of involvement, to draw forth from workers a greater personal interest in the quantity and quality of the product of work. All of this effort is to the good and is an implementation of the encyclical's view that through work man achieves fulfillment as a human being and, indeed, in a sense becomes "more a human being."

Unfortunately, in many instances non-union employers are introducing such programs or giving the appearance of real participation to their employees in an effort to dissuade those employees from joining together in a union. For the most part, such programs will fail in the long run since while they appear to manifest a real concern for worker fulfillment they are, in fact, based on a less admirable desire to maximize profits, and when a conflict between the two eventually arises, as inevitably it will, that conflict will be decided in favor of maximizing profits.[9]

Labor-Management Group: Statement of Purpose (1981)

The U.S. faces a period in its history when noninflationary economic growth and full employment are essential to the maintenance of a free and healthy society.

American labor and business see these as necessary mutual goals to provide our society with new and expanded job opportunities, increased living standards, international competitiveness in an interdependent world and the capacity to meet social commitments.

With these objectives in mind, the Labor-Management Group will meet on a voluntary basis to search for solutions to a wide range of issues.

The principal focus of the Group's discussions will be in the area of economic policy in which its collective experience is widely based. In framing its discussions, the Group is mindful that it is but one of many groups whose opinions may be sought in shaping the nation's policies. The Group's recommendations must consider its obligations to the aspirations of all Americans, including the just demands for equity by minorities, women and those for whom social justice is still a dream.

The national interest requires a new spirit of mutual trust and cooperation, even though management and organized labor are, and will remain, adversaries on many issues.

The uniqueness of America lies in the vitality of its free institutions. Among these, a free labor movement and a free enterprise economy are essential to the achievement of social and political stability and economic prosperity for all. It is destructive to society and to business and organized labor, if in our legitimate adversarial roles, we question the right of our institutions to exist and perform their legitimate functions. In performing these functions, we recognize that both parties must respect deeply held views even when they disagree.

One recognition of the legitimacy of our respective institutions is demonstrated in the process of free collective bargaining. We believe that both the democratic right of employees to determine the issue of representation and the process of collective bargaining must not be threatened by occasions of excessive behavior by employers or unions.

The Group will use the wider relationships its individual members have in the business and labor communities to broaden its knowledge of issues, to improve the overall labor-management climate and to communicate the results of its deliberations to its respective associates.

The complexity of issues suggests the Group may not find complete its views publicly. Otherwise, the participants reserve to themselves the privilege to address issues in their individual capacities.

The group intends to look closely at the issues it knows best and how they are affected by public policy. These are the issues that grow out of our experiences in industries and localities. Further we intend to explore a wide range of issues with particular emphasis on revitalizing the nation's economic base, rebuilding the private and public infrastructure on which our productive capacity as a nation depends, and stimulating safe and efficient means for meeting the nation's energy needs.[10]

Lane Kirkland

Thirty Years After Merger

This convention marks the thirtieth anniversary of the merger of the American Federation of Labor and Congress of Industrial Organizations. . . .

What have we done with the 30 years since?

Despite what our detractors may say to the contrary, we have not been idle, complacent or resistant to change and innovation.

Let me note just a few of the activities and services of the Federation that did not exist prior to the merger, undertaken in response to changing circumstances and needs.

The adoption of an Internal Disputes Plan, successfully addressing a problem that the experts said would surely tear us apart.

The Human Resources Development Institute, expanding our capacity in the field of training, job placement and outreach to those who haven't had a fair chance in life.

The George Meany Center for Labor Studies, elevating the role of education and leadership training in the affairs of the movement and fulfilling an old dream of generations of trade unionists.

The Housing Investment Trust, creating a means of channeling pension and other reserves into the expansion of the national supply of good, union-built, affordable housing.

Labor's Institute of Public Affairs, responding to a widespread demand in our ranks for a consistent presence on television and a full and fair portrayal on that medium, of the role of labor in American life.

Four international institutes, creating a worldwide trade union foreign service to pursue our moral and constitutional obligations to our struggling brothers and sisters overseas, seeking the elevation of their rights and standards and thereby reinforcing our own.

Five support groups—A. Philip Randolph Institute (APRI), Labor

Council for Latin American Advancement (LCLAA), Coalition of Labor Union Women (CLUW), Frontlash and Senior Citizens—to strengthen our alliances with the vital communities they represent.

Four additional departments—the Industrial Union Department, the Public Employee Department, the Department for Professional Employees, and the Food and Allied Services Department—to serve the special needs and strengthen the cooperative work of our affiliates in those sectors.

I suggest to you that this is not the record of a standpat organization mired in complacent self-regard and resistant to change. It is the record of a movement that is open and receptive to new ideas from within or without for new and better ways to serve its members and the human community.

In terms of our organizing mission, there is, as the saying goes, bad news and good news.

The bad news is that our overall growth has been stymied, a new labor force has grown up around us and the trade union share of it has dropped.

The good news is that we have a hell of a lot more people to organize—and we do mean to organize them. . . .

Since 1955, and not counting growth by merger, 15 of our unions have at least doubled their membership, growing from a combined total of 1½ million in 1955 to 4.8 million in 1985. Six unions have more than tripled in size, from a total of 435,000 in 1955 to over 2½ million in 1985. Two unions have multiplied their membership by ten times or more, from a total of 140,000 in 1955 to 1,480,000 in 1985.

We have more than 11 times as many teachers, 10 times as many state, county and municipal workers, 4 times as many pilots, 3½ times as many service employees, 3 times as many actors and artists, and more than twice as many postal workers, fire fighters and communications workers as we did in 1955.

But we have fewer auto workers, fewer steelworkers, fewer garment and textile workers, fewer railroad workers and, alas, many fewer deep sea sailors than we did then.

We have fewer of them because there are fewer of them—not because trade unionism has lost its appeal, nor its necessity, nor because of any delinquency of leadership. I can testify from long and close experience that the leadership of the trade unions in these sectors today is every bit as vigorous, every bit as dedicated, and every bit as creative as in 1955.

What has happened to these unions is a measure of what has happened to America. Let those who revel in their distress consider that the consequences will not be confined to their members only, but will extend across society to the shopkeeper, the landlord and mortgage banker, the farmer and ultimately, I trust, to the most hide-bound politician. This is not just an AFL-CIO problem or a "labor" problem. It is a profound national problem and must be addressed as such.[11]

The Basis for Labor's Interntionalism

Traditional institutions—including corporations and unions—must adapt to changing times or lose their claim to relevance or representivity. I believe the American trade union movement is changing, and not just cosmetically. We are constantly looking for new and better ways of serving our members and reaching out to those not yet organized. In so doing, we are mindful of the strong link between healthy democratic institutions and the cause of freedom itself.

Freedom is a much abused word in our diverse world. We hear censorship, justified in the name of protecting revolutions which, in turn, are defended as the ultimate source of freedom to come.

We hear Third World tyrants and Second World totalitarians deride "procedural rights and freedoms"—counterposing to them allegedly superior economic rights and freedoms.

Others say that democracy as we understand it is a luxury for the rich and an impediment to progress for the developing world. They say much the same about free trade unions.

We are not beguiled by these intellectual convolutions. We think a clearer understanding of freedom is available from those who have been denied it.

Ask the boat people from Indochina. Ask those feeling the tyranny of Castro and the Sandinistas. Ask the hundreds of thousands of Soviet Jews who seek to escape from the twin evils of anti-Semitism and totalitarianism. Ask those who feel the lash of oppression in Chile and Paraguay.

They all have one thing in common. They are denied freedom of association. They are denied the right to band together, to create and control their own institutions, independent of the state, and thereby to protect and advance their interests. They are denied the most important weapon with which to defend all of their other human rights. They stand naked and disarmed before the power of the state.

In the Philippines, we saw what mass organized expression could accomplish. The Trade Union Congress of the Philippines, supported by the AFL-CIO, played a major role in bringing down the Marcos regime.

In South Africa, the most potent force for peaceful democratic change is the black trade union movement, which we also support.

Democracy depends on stable, representative institutions. It depends on the right to organize. It depends on freedom of association.

Just as political democracy sets the framework of procedural rules for resolving societal conflicts, so too did the advent of collective bargaining create a machinery for the peaceable resolution of industrial and workplace disagreements.

This system has been tagged with the deceptive label "adversarial," which conjures up false visions of barricades and social disorder. In fact, it is an essential expression of the principle of contract, which is the glue that holds an open, free and individualistic society, devoid of elements of feudal status, together in relative harmony.

This process cannot work well in an unstable environment. It is difficult to sit across the table from corporate negotiators who are here today and gone tomorrow, or who know or care very little about the long-range problems or needs of their industry, or whose attention is preoccupied by corporate cannibalism.

The full participation of strong trade unions in our system fills a vacuum that the state would otherwise be tempted to fill. Our freedom of association protects the freedom of all Americans—even that of the managerial class.

We want to see strong and effective and free trade unions throughout the world, and we devote considerable resources to that end. We don't want to compete with foreign workers earning 75 cents an hour. We want to compete with the products of foreign workers who earn enough to buy more of their own goods as well as more of ours, and their growing markets as well as ours.

That is why we, together with all of the trade union centers of the OECD [Office for Economic Cooperation and Development] countries, are pressing for the incorporation of a social clause in GATT [General Agreement on Tariffs and Trade] negotiations and agreements requiring the observation of internationally-recognized minimum labor standards as a condition of trading privileges. We have been successful in having that principle included in American trade legislation, and it was partially enforced for the first time in this year's review of the Generalized System of Preferences.

We know that the struggle to build free unions abroad is simultaneously a struggle for human rights and democracy. We feel threatened—economically, politically, and institutionally—whenever workers anywhere are denied their democratic and trade union rights.

That is the basis of labor's internationalism. There we take our stand. We can do no other.[12]

Questions

1. How would you articulate the philosophy of the American labor movement today? Do you think that its philosophy, purposes, and objectives

have changed over the past century? In what respects? How would you characterize its attitudes toward employers, and how have those attitudes changed?

2. How do you account for the change in language between the preambles of the constitutions of the AFL and IWW, on the one hand, and of the CIO of a later date?

3. How would you compare the philosophy of the American labor movement with that of the movements of other Western countries?

4. What role does the philosophy of a labor movement serve within the labor movement? in the larger society? in the international trade union movement? What difference does it make?

5. The AFL-CIO Constitution provides: "No organization officered, controlled or dominated by communists, fascists, or other totalitarians, or whose policies and activities are consistently directed toward the achievements of the program or purposes of the Communist Party, any fascist organization, or other totalitarian movement, shall be permitted as an affiliate of this Federation or any of its state or local bodies." Why is this a concern?

6. George Meany in 1955 articulated his philosophy of the American labor movement and its role in society while projecting the shape of the technology, economy, and polity likely to prevail twenty-five years hence in 1980. In looking ahead to 2015 and beyond, how would you articulate the shape of the environment of the American labor movement and its roles and philosophy? How would your formulation and projection compare to that of George Meany?

Notes

1. See *Report of the Proceedings of the Tenth Annual Convention of the American Federation of Labor,* Detroit, Michigan, December 8–13, 1890. The convention debated whether a charter should be granted to the Central Labor Federation of New York, which had admitted the American Section of the Socialist Labor party to membership. The convention affirmed by a vote of 1,574 to 496 President Gompers's opposition to granting a charter to the Central Labor Federation of New York.

2. Gompers was defeated by John McBride, a United Mine Workers socialist in 1894; the year 1894–1895 was the only year between 1886 and his death in 1925 that Gompers was not president of the Federation.

3. See William Z. Foster, *Misleaders of Labor* (Chicago: Trade Union Education League, 1927).

4. Max M. Kapelman, *The Communist Party vs. the CIO: A Study in Power Politics* (New York: Frederick A. Praeger, 1957).

5. Mr. Hillquit represented the Socialist party of the United States in testimony before the Commission on Industrial Relations, May 21–23, 1914. *The Double Edge of Labor's Sword* (New York: Socialist Literature Company, 1914), pp. 122–124.

6. George Meany, "What Labor Means by 'More,'" *Fortune* (March 1955). Reprinted by permission from FORTUNE Magazine © 1955 Time Inc. All rights reserved.

7. Dave Beck, address at the closing session of the First annual Meeting, Central States Conference of Teamsters, Chicago, April 26, 1954.

8. Center for the Study of Democratic Institutions, *The Corporation and the Union;* an interview by Donald McDonald and J. Irwin Miller with Walter P. Reuther, a series of interviews on the American character (Santa Barbara: The Center for the Study of Democratic Institutions, 1962).

9. Thomas R. Donahue, "A Trade Union Perspective of *Laborem Exercens,* The Encylical of Pope John Paul II" (Washington, D.C.: AFL-CIO, 1982).

10. The Labor-Management Group is made up of eight members of the AFL-CIO Executive Council and eight chief executive officers of companies in The Business Roundtable. See John T. Dunlop, *Dispute Resolution, Negotiation and Consensus Building* (Dover, Mass.: Auburn Publishing Company, 1984, pp. 252–259). This statement was released March 4, 1981.

11. Lane Kirkland, *Proceedings of the Sixteenth Constitutional Convention of the AFL-CIO, Anaheim, California, October 28–31, 1985,* pp. 6–15. (Washington, D.C.: AFL-CIO).

12. Lane Kirkland, excerpt from remarks to the Seventeenth International Management Symposium of the St. Gallen School of Business and Public Administration, St. Gallen, Switzerland, May 18, 1987.

Suggested Reading

Saul Alinsky, *John L. Lewis, An Unauthorized Biography* (New York: G.P. Putnam's Sons, 1949).

David Dubinsky and A. H. Raskin, *David Dubinsky: A Life with Labor* (New York: Simon and Schuster, 1977).

Samuel Gompers, *Seventy Years of Life and Labor,* rev. and ed. Philip Taft and John A. Sessions (New York: E.P. Dutton, 1957).

Samuel Gompers, *The Samuel Gompers Papers,* ed. Stuart B. Kaufman, vol. 1: *The Making of a Union Leader, 1850–86;* vol. 2: *The Early Years of the American Federation of Labor 1887–90* (Urbana: University of Illinois Press, 1986, 1987).

Mark Perlman, *Labor Union Theories in America: Background and Development* (Evanston, Ill.: Row, Peterson, 1958).

Craig Phelan, *William Green: Biography of a Labor Leader* (Albany, N.Y.: State University of New York Press, 1989).

Terrance V. Powderly, *The Path I Trod, Autobiography* (New York: Columbia University Press, 1940.

Archie Robinson, *George Meany and His Time* (New York: Simon and Schuster, 1981).

Studs Terkel, *Working: People Talk about What They Do All Day and How They Feel about What They Do* (New York: Pantheon Books, 1974).

Index

About the Author

John T. Dunlop is Lamont University Professor, Emeritus, at Harvard University, where he has also served as dean of the Faculty of Arts and Sciences. He has had an extensive career in labor relations and government, including membership on the Atomic Energy Labor Relations Panel (1949–1953) and Wage Stabilization Board (1950–1952), as director of the Cost of Living Council (1973–1974), as secretary of labor (1975–1976) and chairman of the Pay Advisory Committee (1979–1980). He has been a chief mediator for many commissions and boards that have handled major labor-management disputes in the coal, railroad, airline, nuclear energy, missile site, and construction industries, as well as in government employment, and he has served as arbitrator in a wide range of industries. Professor Dunlop has written extensively on labor-management relations and on wage determination, labor markets and technological change. He is coordinator of the Labor-Management Group and the Group of Six health care organizations. He received the AFL-CIO's Murry-Green-Meany Award in 1987 and the Work in America Institute Labor-Management Award in 1984 and has been awarded honorary degrees from twelve universities and colleges.